"MANNA-HATIN"

Commerce, looking ever to the future, turns the pages of New York's history.

"MANNA-HATIN"

THE STORY
of
NEW YORK

Published by

THE MANHATTAN COMPANY
NEW YORK

Distributed by

BANK OF MANHATTAN TRUST COMPANY
INTERNATIONAL ACCEPTANCE BANK, INC.
INTERNATIONAL MANHATTAN COMPANY
INCORPORATED

Planned, Designed and Prepared
under the direction of
BREARLEY SERVICE ORGANIZATION
NEW YORK

An Appreciation

IT has been my happy privilege to see and to read an advance copy of *"Manna-hatin,"* *The Story of New York*.

Obviously, this volume is one of special interest to me, for it tells, in a new and stimulating way, the story of my native city—the city which has become the commercial metropolis of the world—the city of which I am proud and honored to be the chief executive by the voice of its people.

It is particularly interesting to learn that the City of New York was one of the original shareholders of The Manhattan Company and was represented on the Company's board of directors for more than a century. Therefore, it seems to me peculiarly appropriate that the Mayor of that city, which is the subject of the book, should voice an appreciation of its contents and of the splendid contribution to public information and understanding which The Manhattan Company has made through the preparation and publication of *"Manna-hatin,"* *The Story of New York*.

I am sure that it will promote a wider knowledge of the city's history and inspire its readers with new pride in the spirit of progress which has won for New York the wonder and admiration of the entire civilized world.

JAMES J. WALKER, *Mayor*
City of New York.

Preface

THE MANHATTAN COMPANY takes pride and pleasure in offering to the public *"Manna-hatin," the Story of New York*. It is not intended as a history, but, as its title implies, a *story* of the development of the city which today is the acknowledged commercial metropolis of the world.

It has seemed appropriate that this contribution to a broader popular understanding of the remarkable progress of New York should be made by an institution which has been continuously identified with it during nearly the entire period of its existence as an American city.

To the many historians whose descriptions of the city's life have been preserved in books, magazines, newspapers and other forms, The Manhattan Company acknowledges a debt of gratitude for the wealth of material upon which it has drawn in the preparation of this volume. It is impossible to enumerate all such sources, but we desire to mention particularly the monumental "Iconography of Manhattan Island," by I. N. Phelps Stokes.

It is the hope of The Manhattan Company that *"Manna-hatin," the Story of New York,* will bring to all readers both pleasure and inspiration and to the present and future citizens of Greater New York new pride in a glorious past, new loyalty to the city in which they live and an eager hope for the still greater and finer city that is to come.

Contents

AN APPRECIATION   PREFACE   FOREWORD

Illustrations

Frontispiece

Foreword

ON a hazy, mid-October afternoon in the year 1928, a huge object, very like a fat, flying slug, moved slowly over the City of New York, and disappeared in the direction of Lakehurst. The sight of an airship was not unusual to the eyes turned up from those streets and windows and housetops, yet the owner of practically every pair of eyes that followed the Graf Zeppelin across the sky must have realized that history was preparing to turn another leaf.

"First commercial aircraft to reach New York via the Atlantic!" shrieked all the extra editions, and the word "commercial" suggested at once how especially important the event would prove to the city that dominates the world's commerce from its lofty watch-towers by the mouth of the Hudson River.

The men who open their morning papers to-day on the banks of almost any other river, whether it be the Thames or the Seine, the Tiber, or even the mysterious Nile, know a great deal about the "commercial metropolis of the world." Sometimes they try to tell its story in the height of the buildings, in the millions of its people who crowd its subways and jam its streets, in the almost incredible figures of the wealth that pours in a golden stream through its markets. Often they forget that the Thames and the Seine, the Tiber and the Nile had been flowing ten and even twenty centuries ere the modest settlements that fringed their banks had grown to famous cities whose towers and palaces have found an abiding place in the history of man.

On that October afternoon of 1928, the adventurous Graf Zeppelin moved slowly above a city that four centuries ago was not even in existence. It must have seemed very much in existence to the Zeppelin passengers as they looked down through the cabin windows. There below, Sandy Hook opened a first gateway from the ocean into the great land-locked harbor, and beyond the narrow channel separating Staten Island from its sister borough of Brooklyn, Manhattan's newest buildings pushed farther than ever through the haze, while its wharves lay like a giant fringe on the waters of a bay fed by thirteen streams and rivers. Had the Zeppelin flown low enough, her passengers might even have heard the whir and grind of the steam shovels, the sound of New York tossing its traditions ruthlessly into the air and devouring its own landmarks.

When the San Franciscan or the Bostonian thinks of New York as "commercial"—which the city most truly is—he often sighs and adds, "But how material!" Yet New York has never been other than careless of its "materials." The face of the city is constantly changing; it is like the magic old Camelot of King Arthur: "built to music . . . built forever, and therefore never built at all!" The only thing that has never changed in the brief three centuries of its building is the tune to which stones have been set in place, torn out, and set again in a new pattern. New York is not a place, after all, but a kind of game, or better, a dream—an adventure; there are no New Yorkers in the sense that there are Londoners, or Parisians, or Romans. Anyone who has a one hundred story imagination, re-inforced with courage, alertness and optimism, finds New York a career.

The biography of this amazing city is necessarily a story of adventure, never a description of the laying out of streets and the preserving of relics. New York's famous men have been famous in some measure as they have caught and reflected the city's spirit.

From the beginning it has been "commercial" in the profounder meaning of that word: in the sense that commerce may be called the handmaiden of civilization itself. Always it has been a highway for commodities from every clime, for travelers from every land, for the cultures of many people. Out of these contacts have come wealth and power, and with them a quicker sympathy, a broader tolerance, and a deeper understanding. Within three centuries a miracle has been wrought. Where stood a few straggling tepees, now towers the great metropolis of a nation, the first commercial city of the world.

The first commercial aircraft to cross the Atlantic moved slowly over New York.

CHAPTER ONE

Only a River!

CAPTAIN HENDRIK HUDSON was disappointed. It was *only* a river, after all, and who cared for rivers when one was looking for a passage to India? Gloomily he gave orders to turn about his clumsy little Dutch craft, "De Halve Maen" (or "Half Moon"), and to sail southward again from Castle Island, near the present City of Albany.

As he made his way back through the heart of a magnificent wilderness he did not realize, of course, that later generations would associate his name with one of the world's most beautiful rivers. Probably his thoughts were very little upon scenery as the Catskill Mountains came into view and disappeared to the westward, as the Highlands rose on either bank, as the broad stretches of Haverstraw Bay and Tappan Zee slipped into the background, and the extraordinary wall of the Palisades frowned at last along the western shore.

Just why this English sea captain had come adventuring into New York harbor in the year 1609 with a little, high, square-sailed Dutch vessel is a curious story in itself, carrying us halfway across the world, and back to the year 1453. For in the year 1453 the Turks captured the city of Constantinople, and when they raised their Star and Crescent over its ancient walls, they set in motion world forces which awakened Europe from the Dark Ages and opened the Golden Age of Adventure.

It was all much simpler than it sounds. Europe had acquired a taste for sugar, spices and other staples which had to be imported from Eastern lands. By 1453 such staples had become a large trade factor, and caravans of slow-stepping camels followed one another across the sands, laden with these much-coveted supplies. Then, suddenly, with the fall of Constantinople, Turkish scimitars barred the way across the desert trade routes. Men were cut off from their "spice islands." Here was a direct challenge to the bold adventurers of Europe. They began to make the long journey around the Cape of Good Hope and across the Indian Ocean, and while many were lost, those who succeeded in bringing back cargoes gained rich rewards.

Then arose the daring Columbus, who believed the world to be round, and conceived the idea of reaching the East by sailing west. Of course he failed, but his failure brought a great continent to the knowledge of Europe and fastened the name "Indian" on a race that had never heard of India.

Other explorers followed, a brilliant and dauntless procession, until gradually the outlines

*"Captain Hendrik Hudson was disappointed;
it was only a river after all!"*

of America began to take form on the maps; yet
the idea persisted that somewhere there must be
a passage which would lead *through* America
and save thousands of miles to the East, if only
it could be found. All up and down the coast
nosed the awkward little craft of hopeful navi-
gators, in search of a doorway to the Orient.

The great natural harbor that lay on the coast
of North America at about 40° latitude could
not hope to remain long unexplored during such
an age of adventure. All races, then as now,
seemed fated to have a hand in the affairs of
New York.

In 1524, the Italian Giovanni Verrazzano,
partly navigator, partly pirate, whose bust may
be seen in Battery Park, entered the harbor,
saw Manhattan Island, and caught a glimpse of
a "great river;" while the Portuguese Estevam
Gomez sighted Sandy Hook the following winter, the one sailing under the orders of King
Francis I of France, and the other exploring for
the Spanish King, Charles V.

Nothing came of these trips, however, save a
tantalizing rumor, traceable to the map drawn
by Verrazzano's brother, Girolamo, that somewhere near 40° latitude, on the coast of America,
lay a great "Sea of Verrazzano."

This rumor helped to make history, as matters
turned out, for it was really one of the factors
that brought Captain Hendrik Hudson's little

"Half-Moon" around the point of Sandy Hook one fine day in September of the year 1609, and lured her through unexplored waters as far as Castle Island. Of course Hendrik Hudson was disappointed. The "Sea of Verrazzano" was a myth, and the hoped-for passageway was only a river after all!

CHAPTER TWO

Hudson Finds "Manna-hatin"

IN A WAY, Captain Hudson deserved some punishment. His very presence in New York Harbor was contrary to all orders from his employers, the Dutch East India Company of Amsterdam.

This great commercial organization had long desired a passage to India for its own trade, and when the States General of Holland offered a purse of twenty-five thousand florins for the discovery of such a route, the East India Company officials sent for the English navigator who had already made something of a reputation for himself as an explorer, and placed the "Halve Maen" in his charge.

"You must sail to the east," they told him, "and seek a northerly passage by way of Nova Zembla. If you don't find it there, you must come home!"

Yet here he was, unmistakably west of the Zuyder Zee!

The fact is that, when it became cold in the region of Nova Zembla and his Dutch crew grumbled, he straightway turned about and headed for the coast of America. Nor were his explorations at about 40° latitude all a matter of chance, for his very good friend, Captain

John Smith—that same adventurer whose life was saved by Pocahontas—had quite recently written him a letter, suggesting that the "Sea of Verrazzano" might be the very passage to India for which he sought.

Accordingly, just eighty-five years after the Italian pirate-navigator had come that way, the "Half Moon" trimmed its square sails and felt its way cautiously into the lower harbor; but on this voyage the exploring vessel was manned by sailors alert to every possibility of commerce. The time was ripe for New York's discovery!

The three weeks that were spent by the captain and crew of the "Half Moon" in trading with the natives and convincing themselves by soundings that they had failed to find a through passage to China, were not without excitement. John Coleman, one of the English sailors, was killed by an arrow while he and a few others were rowing about the lower bay in a small boat, and to him went the distinction of occupying the first white man's grave on Sandy Hook.

Then Hudson in his turn seized two hostages from among the natives who paddled their canoes inquisitively about his ship while it rode at anchor, and on the return trip down the river he was reminded unpleasantly of this act. As the little vessel came abreast of the rocky, wooded island of "Manna-hatin" (so-called by the Indians for "place of the whirlpool" or

"island of mountains" — authorities are not
agreed), out from the tiny strait now known as
Spuyten Duyvil, or "spouting fountain," there
came war canoes filled with Indians who
shouted defiance and showered their arrows
upon the intruder. They were easily beaten off,
but the seeds of a long feud had already been
scattered upon the winds.

In no very happy frame of mind the adventurous captain turned his slow-moving, chunky little craft toward Europe. He carried nothing
with him to show for his waste of time and
money except a few pelts and the well-written
log of the journey. Nor did his disgruntled employers, the East India Company, ever see him
again, for he was detained in Dartmouth Harbor by the English officials, who were not too
well pleased, for their part, that he should serve
under a foreign flag.

The unfortunate Captain Hudson's next journey of exploration proved his last. Seeking to re-
deem his name by finding a passage to the northwest, he passed through Hudson Strait and into
the vast stretches of Hudson Bay, but here the
wretched crew mutinied, threw him and his son
into an open boat, and left them to perish in
those icy solitudes of the far north. It is one of
the strange tricks of Time that his gallant name
still lives, associated with the places of his failure and tragic death.

CHAPTER THREE

Adventuring for Beaver Skins

THE journey of a little handful of Dutch sailors up the Hudson River as far as Castle Island had failed of its object, yet out of that very failure was to grow the commercial City of New York.

To the eyes of Hendrik Hudson's shrewd Dutch mate, as he stood on the deck of the "Half Moon" and watched the island of "Manna-hatin" unfold before him, there could have been no single detail that means "Manhattan" to us. The piers and bridges, the skyscrapers, the rumble and clatter and roar of today's city would have seemed a fantastic dream. In the place of all this stretched a wilderness of quiet, where tangled vines clung to the trees, where wolves and deer moved silently through the forest, and where only the sound of wind among the branches, the lapping of the water, or an occasional bird-call broke the stillness.

Ducks and herons splashed in the waters along the shore, kingfishers darted among the shining leaves, and perhaps a bald eagle from the Palisades soared high overhead. Now and then a canoe would glide from the shelter of a little inlet or from behind one of the wooded islands of the bay, while from the shadowy thickets a startled Indian would show for a moment his painted face and shorn head with its little tuft of hair left growing on one side. It would have seemed to that stolid Dutch mate that only magic could bring about such a transformation as we know. The magic that did bring it about was *Commerce*.

The Dutch East India Company, which had paid all the expenses of this apparently unsuccessful journey, had been organized wholly for commerce, and the spirit of barter and exchange was well reflected in the crew of the "Half Moon." Those practical eyes saw that, while their captain's trail did not lead to the "spice islands," the new-found wilderness appeared to be teaming with wealth in the form of fur. Enough pelts were carried back to show the kind of animals to be found, and the logbook had a good deal to say about them.

Consequently, it was not long before other Dutch craft sailed in through the Narrows for purposes of trade. In 1610, there came a little vessel, supposedly commanded by Hudson's exmate, which proceeded up the river as far as Albany. Its crew bartered with the Indians, who gladly gave them skins of beavers and other animals in exchange for knives and beads. After them came still other traders, among whom were Captain Hendrik Christiaensen and Captain Adrian Block, who presently became partners.

*Captain Block replaced his burned "Tiger" with the
"Onrust," the first vessel to be built in New York.*

While it was with the friendly Indians of the Albany district that the earliest trading was done, a few huts were built among the trees on lower Manhattan, the crude beginnings of a world metropolis. Of course this temporary little encampment was never meant to be home-like, but the men who adventured across the ocean for beaver-skins were ready for any kind of emergency.

Thus, when Captain Block found himself compelled to remain during the winter of 1613 because his ship, the "Tiger," was destroyed by fire, he seems to have been no whit discouraged. The woods began promptly to echo the sounds of hammer and saw, and by spring a new vessel was launched and christened the "Onrust," or "Restless."

Up the East River sailed Block on a tour of investigation, carefully mapping his discoveries. The rushing waters that we know as Hell Gate appeared on his chart as "Hellegat" (which may have been suggested by "Horl-gat" or "channel of the whirlpool"). Once beyond their perils, he sailed in and out of the bays along the Sound, and reached Block Island, to which he gave its name. He discovered that Long Island was indeed surrounded by water, and gave the name "New Netherland" to all the territory lying between the Connecticut and Delaware Rivers.

The "Onrust" set a kind of fashion for exploring in the course of fur-gathering, and other traders began to poke curiously about all the streams and bays in the vicinity, looking for fresh trading grounds which they might claim for themselves. Thus the neighborhood of New York became better and better known—and it was *Commerce* that brought this about. Finally, the States General in Holland issued a proclamation that any merchant might have the sole right, for four voyages a year during a period of three years, to trade with whatever lands were discovered by him.

Thirteen merchants took advantage of this opportunity to form the New Netherland Company with Christiaensen as a director, and thus in an unofficial way, he became the first executive of the vaguely defined province out of which New York was to emerge many years later. However, the unfortunate habit of taking native hostages cut short his rule, for one of the two Indians boys he had carried off to Holland on his first visit proved unforgiving even after he was brought back to his chieftain father, and slew his captor.

By the time the New Netherland Company's charter had expired, its traders had built a rude outpost near Albany, which they called "Fort Nassau," and had concluded an important treaty of peace with the Iroquois. The com-

mercial life of New York was actually beginning to take form, for once in a while a cargo of
skins came down the Hudson River (which the
Dutch merchants called "Mauritius" in honor
of Prince Maurice of Orange) and was shipped
from the little settlement on Manhattan Island
to the buyers in Holland. To this day, there is
a beaver in the seal of New York City, appro-
priately recalling how much these timid fur-
bearers had to do with its founding.

CHAPTER FOUR

Pilgrims, Walloons and Crullers

AT just about the time that a new, powerful Dutch West India Company was using all its political influence to get a charter from the States General, another little clumsy vessel set out for the Hudson River region. Captain Jones knew quite well, as he steered his good ship "Mayflower" out of the English harbor of Plymouth, that his one hundred and two passengers hoped to find their hearts' desire of religious freedom on Manhattan Island.

What a different history might have been New York's had the Pilgrim Fathers and Mothers disembarked with their household goods upon the island of their choice! But the story is told that a Dutch bribe slipped into the hands of the "perfidious Jones" turned the "Mayflower" away from the Dutch trading-post.

"God outshoots Satan sometimes in his own bow," writes one of the Pilgrim descendants, "for had they gone to Hudson's River as before expressed, it had proven very dangerous to them, for although it is a place far more commodious, and the soil more fertile, yet then abounding with a multitude of pernicious savages whereby they would have been in great peril of their lives."

Hence the Pilgrim colony was established on the coast of Massachusetts, and Commerce continued to rule at "Manna-hatin." Its dominion was but a small one. A few huts, a handful of men, a boat at long intervals, some cargoes of pelts—these gave little hint of the millions that were to come.

But world politics were even then beginning to shape the destiny of this canoe-shaped island at the mouth of the Hudson River. Away back in 1606, King James I of England, basing his claim on the discoveries of the Cabots, had made a grant to the Plymouth Company of all land in North America, extending along the coast between 38° and 45° latitude. This, of course, included "New Netherland," where the Dutch traders were so contentedly exchanging beads and other trinkets for rich furs.

Holland, in spite of its size, was powerful on the sea, and was engaged in a struggle for trade advantage with both Spain and England. In the year following the voyage of the "Mayflower," the Dutch West India Company was awarded a charter, that its armed merchantmen might sail forth in pursuit of the richly-laden Spanish galleons. In addition, the directors of the Company were given unlimited power to govern provinces where their vessels traded. In due time the Amsterdam Chamber of the West India Company took over the affairs of New

Netherland, although these seemed of so little importance that the territory was not even mentioned in the charter, and the directors gave the little trading-post at the foot of Manhattan Island its first official name, "New Amsterdam."

But the English claims could not be ignored and it was, therefore, considered sound strategy to meet them by establishing permanent settlements in the disputed territory. Accordingly, thirty families of persecuted Belgian Calvinists, called "Walloons," who offered themselves as colonists, were sent over. Thus the first real residents among the white races were not Dutch, but Belgians.

When they arrived with Captain Cornelis May as director-general, in the ship "Nieu Nederlandt," some of the families were sent up the river to the new Fort Orange near Albany, some to the banks of the Delaware River, and a few to the site of the Brooklyn Navy Yard at Wallabout Bay, which they called "T-Wale-Bocht," or "Bay of The Foreigners."

For a while, the Company seemed to take a lively interest in its adopted child. Cows and farm implements were shipped over, and more colonists—simple people who were too much occupied with building their houses to worry at first about government detail. An engineer, Kryn Fredericksz, was presently dispatched with his rule and compass, and made a map showing how Fort New Amsterdam should be built, with its star-shaped bastions, and at what point on the present State Street a windmill's broad sweep should rise. There was also to be a loft above the horsemill near South William and Pearl Streets of today, where on a Sunday the colonists could sit among the grain sacks and worship in the Dutch Reformed fashion.

Then, too, Sebastian Krol came over to serve as "marriage clerk," as temporary director and as "comforter of the sick." How important a person he was in the little community we may partly guess from the tradition that our modern "cruller" takes its name and form from a Dutch delicacy called "krolyer" after the good man who seems to have carried a supply of these about with him in cheering the sick!

However, these early colonists were fated to need many forms of comfort and cheer beside the humble cruller during the first years of their struggle with the wilderness.

CHAPTER FIVE

The Indians Sell "Manna-hatin"

THE English were not at all pleased with the colony of New Amsterdam so impudently planted within the limits of the King James' grant, for the Dutch showed no signs of leaving.

Both England and Holland desired to avoid war, although neither wished to relinquish its claim, and thus for years the neighboring people of New England and New Netherland were kept in a feverish state of bluffing each other about who owned the land.

The West India Company must have felt that a gesture of ownership on its part would improve matters. Therefore, when a new director, Peter Minuit, was sent over in 1626, he came with instructions to purchase "Manna-hatin" from the Indians.

Real estate operators since Minuit's time have often thought wistfully of that first bargain—the entire island of Manhattan for sixty guilders' worth of trinkets, or twenty-four dollars! But it now appears that the Canarsie Indians, from whom Minuit made his purchase, were not so simple-minded as they seemed, for they took payment for something they did not really own. This tribe, along with the Montauks, the Rock-

aways and others, dwelt on Long Island, merely
trading on Manhattan, and their trickery made
it necessary for the white man to buy part of the
island over again from the tribes living near
Washington Heights.

Still more crafty were the Raritans of
"Staaten Eylandt" (so named for the States General), for the records show that Staten Island
was sold by these Indians no less than six times!

The settlement over which Peter Minuit
ruled was very small, and huddled near the fort,
before which a wide "plain" opened out on the
site of our present Bowling Green. It is true that
the Heere Gracht (now Broad Street) had little
bridges spanning its canal, giving the town
somewhat the appearance of old Amsterdam,
but progress was lacking. No one was permitted
to trade on his own account; help was scarce and
the better classes did not come over from Holland because conditions at that time were more
prosperous at home.

Then, in 1628, the West India Company committed a grave error: it promised huge grants of
land to wealthy Hollanders who would bring
out fifty colonists at their own expense. These
great land-owners, called "patroons," became almost little kings on their own estates, and were
able to rule their colonists with an iron hand by
reason of the life and death privileges permitted
in their charters.

*Peter Minuit purchased "Manna-hatin" from the Canarsie
Indians for twenty-four dollars' worth of trinkets.*

From the patroon grant made at a later date to Adrian Van der Donck, the present site and name of Yonkers can be traced in "Yonkheer's Landt," or the "Young Lord's Land."

But with one or two exceptions, the patroon system did not turn out well, for the land-owners grew haughty, and quarreled with the governors of New Amsterdam, while the people they ruled became sullen under their restrictions.

Peter Minuit was a wise and kindly governor, insisting that the Indians be treated with fairness. This humane policy did not prevent a sad tragedy that was to bring a heavy retribution. Three servants of the West India Company happened one day to encounter an old Indian walking with his nephew in the woods by the Fresh Water Pond, later called the "Collect," where the Tombs Prison now stands. The cowardly fellows set upon the old man, robbing him of the beaver skins he was carrying to the post, and beating him to death. The nephew escaped through the forest and waited patiently during twelve long years for his chance to take vengeance. When it finally came, the massacre that resulted was costly payment for the life of one old Indian.

CHAPTER SIX

A Wedding and a Tragedy

THE captain of the Dutch trading-vessel "Eindracht" must have been a crusty old fellow with little romance in his heart. He was not very far-sighted, either, but of course he could not have suspected that an unsympathetic word of his would finally result in the loss of New Amsterdam to the Dutch. Yet his "no" was like striking a match to a fuse.

The "Eindracht," carrying furs from New Amsterdam to Holland, had put into the English port of Plymouth, and would have sailed out again without adventure had the pilot not asked the captain for a delay in order that he might marry. When the captain refused, the pilot saw a way out in appealing to the provost of the port to detain the ship, suggesting that a Dutch vessel had no business to be trading in English territory.

We do not know if the pilot's marriage turned out happily or not, but we do know that the English seized the "Eindracht" and that the matter got into the courts, calling official attention very sharply to the fact that the Dutch were holding territory claimed by the English under the terms of the King James' grant to the Plymouth Company in 1606.

The English decided to push forward their colonizing until the time should come for a contest. In 1635, King Charles I made a grant of Long Island to Alexander, Lord Stirling, and more and more English settlers crossed the seas to dispute with the Dutch the rights to New Netherland. There was still a great deal of room, but as the two peoples had come with the intention of elbowing each other, it was not long before they began to do so. The English planted settlements in the eastern end of Long Island and pushed westward. The Dutch settled the western end and for a time sat tight. They watched each other closely, like the jealous rivals they were, but it was years before the clash came.

Meanwhile, the Dutch continued to set up a "little Holland" on Manhattan Island. They built tall, gabled Dutch houses near their Dutch canal, smoked their long-stemmed pipes on the wooden benches by the side of their Dutch doorways, and argued emphatically in guttural Dutch words. They listed to the sermons of Dominie Bogardus in the little wooden church that succeeded the horsemill loft, and they sent their boys and girls to Adam Roelantsen, the first school-teacher. Adam was not a huge success at teaching, and presently tried to piece out his income by renting a "bleaching ground" beside the pond where the buxom Dutch maids washed the household linen. The little country path

A Wedding and a Tragedy

Down Maiden Lane to the washing-pool came the buxom Dutch maids, carrying their bundles of linen.

down which they came with their bundles, winds today between tall skyscrapers, yet it still bears the name of "Maiden Lane."

Wouter Van Twiller had become governor following the recall of Minuit, and while he made little money for the company, he did pretty well for himself. Among other properties, he purchased Nut Island from the Canarsie Indians, establishing there a "bouwerie" or farm which he cultivated at the Company's expense, and to his own profit. Therefore it became known as Governor's Island. Finally the Company wearied of this one-sided thrift, and recalled Van Twiller, only to send out in his place

a meddlesome little busybody named Kieft, who
managed during the years of his rule to bring
disaster upon the entire colony.

Nearly all of William Kieft's policies were
unwise, but it was in his dealings with the
Indians that he did the greatest harm. In 1640
some pigs were stolen on Staten Island, by servants of the West India Company as it appeared
later. Without proving his suspicions, Kieft at
once sent an expedition against the innocent
Raritans. In the bitter feelings stirred up by
this injustice, the Weckquaesgeek Indian boy
who had fled from his uncle's assailants by the
Fresh Water Pond, at last found his chance to
strike. His victim was Claes Swits, a wheel-
wright who lived near Turtle Bay. There was a
witness to his act, and Kieft demanded that his
tribe surrender him. This they refused to do,
and the long years of Indian warfare began.

It was in 1643, during this period of terror,
that Kieft was responsible for the most dastardly
and bloody act in the history of New York. The
powerful Mohawks came down the river to collect tribute from the Weckquaesgeeks, and as
they came armed, the weaker tribe fled for protection to Pavonia and Corlear's Hook. Their
very trust in the white man betrayed them, for
in the dead of night Kieft sent his soldiers to
slaughter the refugees—women and children as
well as the braves.

David De Vries, a patroon of Staten Island, and a man of great wisdom in Indian affairs, had done his best to prevent the massacre, and all night he sat in the fort, helpless and horror-stricken, listening to the cries that drifted from the Jersey shore across the ominous stillness of the river. Toward morning an Indian and his wife, who had escaped from what they thought were the Mohawks, came knocking at the gate, pleading to be taken in. De Vries sadly told them the truth, and helped them to rejoin the Weckquaesgeek tribe.

The penalty for Kieft's act was shared by the whole colony. Eleven tribes of Indians went on the warpath, and the shores resounded with their yells. Before long Staten Island as well as Pavonia lay in ashes about the mutilated bodies of white men. Only fortified New Amsterdam and a few settlements on Long Island were left in the possession of the white intruders.

As for De Vries and the friends who fled to his manor for refuge during the devastation of Staten Island, they were most dramatically saved by the appearance of the very Indian whom he had helped to escape from the fort on the night of the massacre.

Kieft's efforts at making peace were unsuccessful, and at last Captain John Underhill, an English officer who had settled at Stamford, came to the rescue of the colony. His raid on the headquarters of the Connecticut Indians brought the bloody period to a close, and New Amsterdam was saved—but not for Kieft. The citizens had addressed a "Remonstrance" to the States General of Holland and the West India Company was forced to recall the unpopular governor. William Kieft never reached Holland to answer the charges, however, for the ship "Princess," on which he and Dominie Bogardus took passage in 1647, sank in the English Channel, and both men were drowned.

CHAPTER SEVEN

"Old Silver Nails" Arrives

IT WAS in the spring—in the time of hope and fresh beginnings—that the inhabitants of New Amsterdam crowded around the little landing-place near the fort to wave their broad hats in welcome to the new governor. Their indifference to civic affairs was fast disappearing, and with more than idle curiosity they watched the figure that stepped off the boat from Curacao—a haughty figure that moved with the air of a prince in spite of its silver-banded wooden leg. New Amsterdam had probably heard of the wooden leg, for Governor Peter Stuyvesant had earned it during an enviable military career, and the current nickname of "Old Silver Nails" was one that doubtless offended the stern old soldier least of all.

The smooth-shaven face suggested strength, efficiency, and a scholarly intelligence. There was, besides, a hopeful note in the speech he made to his enthusiastic new subjects on this occasion. "I shall be a father to you," he promised; and how the Dutch must have waved their broad-brimmed hats at that!

Very soon, however, the discouraged colonists learned that fatherly conduct meant stamping his wooden leg at them, flying into rages when wise advice ran counter to his policies, and, in short, letting them have their own way about nothing whatever.

Fortunately, the Stuyvesant way was a good one in most respects, and between the years 1647 and 1664 he managed to bring about many reforms in New Netherland. The Dutch houses, with their brass knockers and curious gabled ends of checkered black and yellow bricks, were kept spotlessly clean, but the narrow, crooked little streets that often followed the original cow paths about the lower part of the island, were filthy, and these Stuyvesant promptly ordered to be cleaned, and in some cases straightened out into dignified thoroughfares.

Many taverns had opened here and there in the settlement, for a large part of the population was engaged in brewing. The new governor now took these in hand, making rules about the length of supper parties, and the charges for meals and other accommodations.

Instead of learning to read and write, the boys and girls of New Amsterdam were helping with the work, and this condition of affairs shocked Governor Stuyvesant, who had children of his own. Through his encouragement, education began to prosper, and by the early '60's the prestige of the Dutch colony's Latin school under Ægidius Luyck, a former tutor of the Stuyvesant children, had spread beyond the boundaries of New Netherland, and was attracting pupils from many of the neighboring New England towns.

Governor Stuyvesant found a rather scattered population at the beginning of his rule. Under Kieft, most of the land on Long Island had been purchased from the Canarsies, the first real estate deal in the present borough of Brooklyn having been the exchange of Coney (from the Indian "Conynge" or "Rabbit") Island, for a single pound of shot.

Religious persecution had driven many English settlers into the present Queens Borough and Westchester County from New England, for the West India Company recognized tolerance as a sound commercial policy, and no witches were ever burned on New York soil. The family of Ann Hutchinson had accordingly settled in the region of New Rochelle; the Pell family had come to give their name to Pelham; at Gravesend a grant was given the English Lady Moody; while Kieft had permitted one Thomas Stiles and his associates to incorporate the town of Flushing (Vlissingen). These growing little communities kept their English customs, but they submitted in a half-hearted way to the rule of a Dutch governor.

Dutch farms, or "bouweries," had sprung up here and there in the western part of Long Island, and a few houses clustered together at what is now the Brooklyn end of the Fulton Ferry, while near the close of Kieft's term, Jan Evertsen Bout and a few others made a permanent settlement about a mile farther inland. This was incorporated as "Breuckelen," or "broken ground," and when the English later altered the name to "Brookland," it more nearly suggested the modern Brooklyn.

Over on Staten Island there had been attempts made to start a village called "Oude Dorp," or "Old Town," and Patroon Melyn in 1640 had set up at the Narrows a kind of marine telegraph in the form of a white flag that warned of approaching vessels, but most of the settlements made before Stuyvesant's time were wiped out by Indian raids.

On Manhattan, a grant to Dr. de la Montagne formed the germ of modern Yorkville, and farther north, the present Bronx Borough was being farmed by the energetic Jonas Bronck, from whom it takes its name.

The New Netherland over which Governor Peter Stuyvesant was sent to rule in 1647 was thus very far from being a compact, prosperous little community. Kieft's mistakes had made the colonists suspicious of all rulers; the menace of Indian massacre still hovered in the air, while the hour of contest between the English and the Dutch over the possession of the land drew nearer and nearer.

CHAPTER EIGHT

How Wall Street Began

SOME one has pointed out that Stuyvesant's name means "he who kicks up a dust," and certainly it was not long before the stamping of his wooden leg set in motion a series of most important events for the entire colony.

Melyn and his fellow patroon Kuyter, of Staten Island, complained that they had been ruined by Kieft's policy toward the Indians.

"What!" exclaimed Stuyvesant; "do you presume to criticize an ex-governor?" And he promptly banished them.

This high-handed act awoke such a mutter of protest from the inhabitants of New Netherland that Stuyvesant was forced to appoint nine men as councillors. Almost from the first, the council meetings must have been lively affairs, for there was a great deal to worry about. The boundary disputes with the English were growing more serious, and all that the West India Company would do about the matter was to advise the colonists to live as peaceably as possible. The Swedes, moreover, had settled on the Delaware River in territory claimed by the Dutch, and they refused to leave.

Then, quite unexpectedly, the banished patroon, Melyn, returned in triumph from Holland, bringing a summons for the governor to cross the seas and appear before the States General. The humiliated Stuyvesant sent his lawyer to represent him, instead, and the Council of Nine Men seized the occasion to send Van der Donck, the "Jonkheer," with a "Representation of New Netherlands," telling *their* story.

The States General listened to everyone—at great length—and then did nothing about the matter, but the hearing attracted much attention, and was the first wide advertising the little colony had ever received. All Holland heard about its resources and opportunities, and the result was a higher type of immigration.

The new-comers were not in a strict sense immigrants; they were for the most part well-to-do merchants, who transplanted themselves, their luxurious house-furnishings, their whole manner of living, to the new soil. French Huguenots of culture and refinement added a grace and vivacity to the life of Manhattan Island, and from this period, New Amsterdam became an aristocratic little town.

Governor Stuyvesant was a very busy person in those days, stumping angrily about, now quarreling with his council, now threatening the Swedes, now the English, and ordering his cannon out to put the Schuylers and Dyckmans in their places at the powerful little patroon grant of Rensselaerswyck near Albany. New Netherland was thus taking itself very seriously, all unmindful of the fact that across the seas a measure was being adopted that was bound gravely to affect its future. In 1651 the British Parliament passed the Navigation Act whose purpose was to crush the commercial supremacy of the Dutch.

The seal of New Amsterdam.

The West India Company's first reaction was to give a hasty sort of peace offering to its neglected "trading-post." On February 2, 1653, New Amsterdam received a municipal form of government; the city's first seal, with its beaver and crosses, made its appearance, and the town tavern at Coenties' Slip was given a thorough housecleaning to fit it up for new dignity as the Stadt Huys or City Hall.

Still high-handed, Stuyvesant did away with the bother of elections, and appointed all officials himself! Bickerings and disputes broke out afresh over this; yet in 1654, when word came that Cromwell, who had overthrown the English monarchy, was arming a fleet for the capture of the Dutch colony, all factions united in the terror of the moment.

A fence had been constructed on the site of Wall Street to keep out wandering cows, and this was now made into a stout blockade, or wall, from which the street later took its name. Then suddenly, in the midst of these defense measures, peace was declared, and all was safe for a while.

The Jewish race had long ranked high in European commerce, but until this time patroon rights had been denied to any one of them. The first group came over with Asser Levy, but it took them three years to overcome bigotry and gain permission to buy land, or even to serve with other citizens on the burgher watch that patrolled the town nightly, calling out the hour and weather at each corner.

The Dutch Reformed Church, with Dominie Megapolensis in charge at New Amsterdam, was still the official guide for the religious life of the colony. In Kieft's time the little wooden chapel had been replaced by a stone building known as the Church of St. Nicholas. This benevolent saint had been the figurehead on the first immigrant ship to reach New Amsterdam, and became the patron saint of the town as well as the church. The congregation has continued under the same name, and the Church of St. Nicholas stands today at the corner of Fifth Avenue and Forty-eighth Street.

As the Indian girl reached for one of his prize peaches,
Van Dyck seized his musket.

The first Dutch church on Long Island was
established in 1654 at Midwout (Flatbush) and
when the Brooklynites protested at having to
journey so far for their sermons, Stuyvesant
helped them to pay the salary of a pastor of their
own on condition that he would preach on Sunday afternoons at the governor's own "bouwerie." This farm extended from the present
Bowery to the East River, bounded rather ir-
regularly on the north and south by the lines of
Eighth Street and Fourth Street. The chapel
which Stuyvesant built for Dominie Selyns stood
on the site of today's St. Mark's-in-the-Bowery,
where the bones of the old governor have found
an appropriate resting-place.

However, in 1655, "Old Silver Nails" was
very much alive. He finally routed the Swedes
from the Delaware by leading an expedition
against them himself, and hurried back from
that campaign to meet a tragedy in New Amsterdam that his own vigorous presence there
might have averted.

Van Dyck, a town official who should have
known better, had let his quick temper betray
him into a stupid and brutal act. He was very
proud of his fine peaches, and one evening when
he observed an Indian woman reaching for one,
he straightway reached for his musket and killed
her. All the old native resentment awoke, and
by the next evening nine hundred Indian war-

riors had assembled at Inwood and were soon making their way down the river. Their stealthy arrival in New Amsterdam filled the inhabitants with terror, but for the time being a parley with their sachems resulted in the Indians withdrawing to Staten Island. When it became dark again, however, they returned, killed Van Dyck, and then leaping into their canoes, hastened across to the Jersey shore and back to Staten Island, where they slaughtered or carried into captivity over two hundred persons.

Stuyvesant met this emergency with great wisdom. "It becomes us to reform ourselves," he said, and refused to wage war in retaliation. In the nervousness that followed the savage outbreak, a proclamation was issued forbidding the occupation of farms in the Bronx. This checked the development of that region, and the whole colony felt the need of more agricultural activity. Accordingly, in 1658, when fear was over, the governor offered a ferry to Long Island and a clergyman to any twenty-five families that would plant a village in the northern part of Manhattan. This resulted in the founding of "New Harlem," named in memory of old Haarlem in Holland, a district that was destined to change its character many times in the course of the centuries, as new nationalities and new races should come and go in the great moving tides of its population.

CHAPTER NINE

Customs and Costumes

TROUBLES with the Indians continued until the end of the Dutch rule, but they centered about the distant village of Esopus, in the Hudson highlands. To New Amsterdam was left a brief period of peace in which to improve itself. A few cobblestone pavements were laid, the first one changing the name of Brewer Street, so-called from the Van Cortlandt brewery, to Stone Street. Along the "Strand," or shore, which has since retreated from the East River to become Pearl Street, fine new stone houses were built, and gardens were cultivated where bright tulip beds and little summer-houses made a proper setting for the colorful Dutch costume. Governor Stuyvesant had his country home on his bouwerie, but gave up his official residence in the fort to build a great mansion of hewn stone, christened "Whitehall" by the English in later years. The name survives in the present Whitehall Street, at the foot of which it stood. The Verplanck family erected a spacious home on Bridge Street, as did Hendrick Kip, and the Brevoort bouwerie was laid out along the western side of Bouwerie Lane, the path leading to the Stuyvesant farm on the East River.

Social life was very gay, especially in the last four or five years of Stuyvesant's rule. The Dutch nature was free and joyous, and prosperity was general. Many of the citizens were adventurous traders whose ships brought back rich prizes from all parts of the world, making life luxurious; nothing was too good for daily use. Commerce had so attracted the people of different races that after 1643 it was necessary to have an official interpreter, and by 1660, eighteen languages were spoken on the streets of New Amsterdam.

All this kept New York from getting in a rut. Its commercial foundation had made the city what it continues to be, a meeting-place of nations, and from this exchange of ideas and intermingling of customs, there has come a quickening of men's imaginations. In spite of its vast growth, New York has never "grown up"; it has kept its youthful spirit of joyous energy, interest in novelty, and love of adventure.

This was already apparent in the little city of the seventeenth century. Children listened to the strange tales of the Indians and of the African slaves and learned from their parents the merry games of Holland. The ideas of three continents mingled thus in their young minds, and gave them a peculiar freedom of vision which is bearing fruit today in Greater New York. Even some of the games have survived in

part. Our Christmas Eve celebration, with a
portly Santa Claus handing presents from a tree,
descends from the children's festival of St.
Nicholas, and the Thanksgiving custom of letting the children roam the streets in masquer-
ade has almost forgotten its origin in the Shrove
Tuesday game.

There were many pleasant customs among
those early New Yorkers—their May Day dancing about the tall pole in the fort, their skating
parties, weddings, christenings, and the Kermis,
or fair, which made the Strand alive from
Whitehall to Broad Street with the display of
farm produce, with puppet shows, with trumpet
calls, and the shrill cries of the vendors.

Among all these customs, perhaps the one to
which later times attached the greatest sentiment is the habit of making New Year's Day
calls. On that day of days, the New Amsterdam
maiden would wear her best jeweled head-dress,
her most delicately pleated ruff, and seated in
the "front room" among her family's treasures
of heavy silver and dull pewter, she would await
the coming of those youths who were socially
eligible. Many of their names are familiar today: de Peyster, Van Cortlandt, Schuyler, de
Sille, Roosevelt, Bayard, de Lancey. Decked
out as if for a Hals or a Rembrandt portrait,
the New Amsterdam youth went on his way to
pay the New Year calls down streets whose

names were more picturesque than those of to-day—for Pie Woman's Lane has become Nassau Street; the little path that followed the windings of Minitie Water is today Minetta Lane, and Gramercy Square has lost all memory of the old bouwerie of the "Krommessie" or crooked knife.

CHAPTER TEN

"Silver Nails" Surrenders

IT IS a pity that a bright reflection of Dutch fairs and weddings and tea parties cannot complete the picture of events up to 1664. But New York comprises more than the Island of Manhattan, and over on Staten Island and Long Island matters were quite different. Only one Huguenot village at Stony Brook relieved the desolation of Staten Island, and Stuyvesant's personal religious bigotry, so contrary to the tolerant policies of the West India Company, brought misery to eastern Long Island.

This was all the more unfortunate because the time was fast approaching when the loyalty of the new little towns all over Long Island would be needed by the Dutch governor. Their growth had been rapid; Jacques Cortelyou had bought a tract of land from the Indians for six coats, six chisels, six axes, six kettles, six small looking-glasses, twelve knives, and twelve combs, and in 1661 Stuyvesant gave a charter for New Utrecht, the town that sprang from his purchase. Rust Dorp, or "Quiet Village," was the name chosen by the founders of another settlement, but it is the little Indian "jameco," or beaver pond, nearby, that gave it its present name of Jamaica. Stuyvesant granted charters to Flush-

ing, Newtown, Long Island City and Hempstead, but what good-will he might have won by
these measures, he lost by his bigotry.

Quakers had migrated in large numbers to
Long Island, but a proclamation by the governor forbade the holding of meetings. When it
was reported that the Bowne house (which still
stands in Flushing) had harbored these forbidden gatherings, Stuyvesant promptly banished
its owner to Holland. Flushing was no less
resolute than the governor, however, and when
one Henry Townsend was sentenced to a fine and
imprisonment for preaching contrary to the
proclamation, thirty of its citizens boldly signed
their names to a protest, and in spite of Stuyvesant's threatened retaliation, refused to carry
out the sentence on the victim.

Bigoted cruelty overstepped itself in the case
of Robert Hodgson, arrested by Stuyvesant for
preaching in Hempstead, and the result was a
ban on all religious persecution. The unfortunate man was kept without food, was suspended
by his thumbs in his cell, and from time to time
brutally lashed, until the governor's own sister
interceded for him. Then came an order from
the West India Company, sharply rebuking
Stuyvesant, and closing the brief chapter of
religious intolerance.

The West India Company could little afford
to lose ground. In 1660, when the Restoration

placed Charles II on the English throne, one of
the first acts of his parliament was to revive the
old Navigation Act, making it necessary for all
English commerce to be carried on in English
ships. This act could not be enforced so long
as a commercial colony like New Amsterdam
held the key position on the Eastern coast and
engaged in a lively trade with New England
under another flag. The passage of the act, therefore, doomed the independence of the little
Dutch outpost.

As English boundary disputes grew more
pressing, Stuyvesant wrote an urgent remonstrance to the West India Company, asking that
a definite charter be sought from the States General, and also that adequate protection be given
the colony. Guns and soldiers never came, but
in 1663 the States General *did* pass a belated
grant of the disputed soil. At the same time, the
Dutch ambassador asked the British Parliament
to ratify a so-called "Hartford Treaty" that
Stuyvesant had drawn up with New England,
establishing the border line between the two
colonies. The king's answer was an immediate
grant to his brother, James, Duke of York and
Albany, of all the territory claimed as the Dutch
New Netherland!

New Amsterdam had just gone through a year
of calamities; a flood had destroyed the crops;
there had been an earthquate and an epidemic

"Old Silver Nails" was persuaded not to fire and New Amsterdam surrendered to the English.

of smallpox among the settlers, and a massacre by the Indians at Esopus had terrorized the entire colony of New Netherland.

Now, as a hint of fresh disaster, came the news that the Duke of York had dispatched a force under Colonel Richard Nicolls for the taking over of his new territory.

The arrival of the squadron found the English settlers of Long Island awaiting their fellow-countrymen with open arms, and willing to furnish volunteers to aid in the capture of the Dutch possession.

Stuyvesant had four hundred soldiers in the fort, and a scanty twenty-four barrels of water. In spite of these odds, he determined to defend the city, and when a letter came from Nicolls with most generous terms of surrender, he refused to show it, but tore it up in the presence of the council, for fear they might insist upon accepting its conditions. However, the time was past for letting "Old Silver Nails" have things all his own way. His nephew, Nicholas Bayard, then serving as secretary to the province, carefully pieced the torn letter together and showed it to the burgomasters. At once they drew up a petition asking for surrender, and among the signatures the proud old governor found the name of his own son.

Even then he stood ready to resist the enemy. Into the upper bay sailed the English frigates, their guns leveled at the fort, and the anxious watchers on the ramparts saw him about to give the order "Fire!" The very eyes of the garrison must have seemed hostile to him, and suddenly the fierce old soldier's resolution broke down. Dominie Megapolensis led him away, and New Amsterdam passed without resistance into the custody of an English duke.

The terms of surrender were agreed upon at Stuyvesant's bouwerie on September 6, 1664. There was no question of national loyalty involved, for the town had belonged, not to Holland, but to a Dutch trading company, which for the last thirty years had done little more than send over tyrannical directors and complaints about revenue.

CHAPTER ELEVEN

"Manna-hatin" Becomes English

THE little outpost that Commerce had founded and maintained so stoutly through an adventurous half-century, was at once re-christened by its English captor. Under Duke James, New Amsterdam became New York, borrowing its name from the duke's own ancient cathedral city of York, once the seat of Roman government in Britain. At the same time that it received its modern name, its boundaries were extended to take in all of Manhattan. Long Island (officially known for many years as "Nassau Island"), Staten Island and the present Westchester County were combined by the duke into "Yorkshire." Jersey he bestowed upon two of his favorites.

His appointment of Richard Nicolls as governor-general over the new province was a most fortunate one. So tactful and popular was his rule that even the peppery Stuyvesant became his friend, and often entertained him at the very bouwerie where terms of Dutch surrender had been signed.

In fact, response to the first English governor was instantaneous. Hardly had he raised his country's flag over the little Manhattan town with its fifteen hundred inhabitants than the local exchange registered its first violent fluctuation. Wampum went up 400 per cent. New York, even in its infancy, was learning to trade on the news of the day.

At first, everything looked encouraging. On June 12, 1665, the ducal charter establishing the English form of municipal government in place of the Dutch, was proclaimed by Nicolls. Among other rights, it permitted trial by jury, and while the new town officers, the mayor, sheriff, and aldermen were to be appointed by the governor rather than elected, Nicolls delayed opposition by keeping in office such men as Nicholas Bayard, Johannes de Peyster, Jacob Kip and Olaff Van Cortlandt, who had served under Stuyvesant. The farm of the West India Company, which forms part of the present Trinity Church property on Broadway, was confiscated on the pretext that its directors had "inflicted all sorts of injuries on His Majesty's subjects." This flattered the citizens, who at first did not mind that all laws were made by the governor, and were merely submitted to their representatives for ratification.

But the stupid avarice of Duke James, to whom his new possessions meant only an opportunity for exploitation, brought a change in the attitude of the people. Even the Puritans who had begun to come to Long Island about 1665 to seek a quiet refuge in its farm lands, resented

the exorbitant fees that were demanded for new
land patents.

Another cause of friction had its origin in the
failure of the English to appreciate the character of the people of the colony. Francis Lovelace, who came over as governor to succeed the
well-loved Nicolls, was surprised to find that
the people of New York had the "breeding of
courts." They, in turn, fiercely resented being
treated as inferiors by the British.

New York at this time was peopled by a mix-
ture of races. It was far from democratic, and
those who composed its "upper crust" were ex-
ceedingly proud of their distinguished Huguenot or Dutch descent. They were used even to
greater luxury than many of the English wealthy
class, and were keenly sensitive to the patroniz-
ing airs of the "stay-at-homes." Thus, from the
beginning, there was much misunderstanding between the English who were reared among the
traditions of Britain, and the race that inherited
the commercial traditions of New York.

CHAPTER TWELVE

New York Wins Staten Island

SINCE the days of Kieft, when Indians thirsting for revenge began to choose its lonely farms and woodlands for their most frequent attacks, Staten Island had led a rather dramatic existence. Now, under the Duke of York, the whole question of its relationship to neighboring territory for centuries to come was settled by the adventures of a single day.

Both New Jersey and New York wanted Staten Island. There had been much dispute about the boundaries, and it was agreed that New York should have all the islands in the harbor that could be circumnavigated in twenty-four hours. Staten Island, separated from New Jersey by only the narrow Kill van Kull and Arthur Kill, might never have joined Greater New York as the Borough of Richmond had it not been for skillful Captain Charles Billop and his sloop, the "Bentley." Sailing around Staten Island in twenty-four hours seemed one of those things that "couldn't be done"—but doing the impossible is the test of a New Yorker. Accordingly, Captain Billop tacked and veered; the little "Bentley" strained at its canvas, and between them Richmond Borough was saved for Greater New York. The captain was rewarded by a vast manor grant at Tottenville to which he gave the name of "Bentley" in commemoration of his sloop.

Governor Lovelace made the last, and sixth, purchase of Staten Island from the Indians, and in his time the island's real progress began. Surveyors were sent over, and by 1700 at least two hundred families had settled there.

Other parts of the province forged ahead, as well. A ferry was established to the Bronx at about 125th Street, and from lower Manhattan Island a narrow wagon road was laid to the village of Harlem, encouraging little taverns to spring up along its route. On the present site of Garden City a race-course was built, called the Newmarket, which became a sporting centre for all the colonies.

Before long, the bustling merchant ships from over seas brought word that England, Sweden and Holland had formed the Triple Alliance, and this fact served to bind New York's inhabitants into closer friendship with each other. A club of prominent families began to meet twice a week in each other's homes, and to hold a series of formal "affairs" that set the aristocratic tone of New York society for generations.

There was a beginning of cooperation among the merchants, as well, for early in 1670 Governor Lovelace opened a Merchants' Exchange. This first "curb market" met each Friday morn-

*Captain Billop sailed around Staten Island
and won it for New York.*

ing at the bridge over the Heere Gracht, or
"Gentlemen's Canal" (which still flowed down
our present Broad Street)—much to the disgust,
we may imagine, of the small boys who were
forbidden to use their sleds on that especially
fine, steep hill leading to the bridge.

Then, once again England and Holland went
to war and the threat of Dutch recapture stirred
little New York to a high pitch of excitement.
Governor Lovelace felt that he and Governor
Winthrop of Massachusetts should keep each
other informed of events in such a time of peril,
and consequently the first postal service between
the colonies grew out of the moment's need. It
was not elaborate. John Archer set out for Boston by horseback, with his packet of letters; he
marked his route carefully on the trees, and in
due time returned with Governor Winthrop's
neatly inscribed answers.

However, in spite of all his efforts to keep on
the alert, Lovelace was finally caught napping.
When the Dutch fleet sailed up the bay, on
August 9, 1673, the governor was visiting in
New Rochelle, and Captain Manning, who was
in charge of the fort, could do nothing in its defense. His guns had been spiked by Dutch
sympathizers, and after an hour of bombarding
on the part of Admiral Evertsen, commanding
the Dutch attack, Manning surrendered as Stuyvesant had done, without firing a shot.

For this act his sword was later broken over his head. He retired in disgrace to his estate on "Hog Island" which, upon his death, took its name from his son-in-law, Robert Blackwell. Today a place of gloomy prisons, it is officially known as "Welfare Island."

In the meanwhile, New York had become "New Orange" under the brief return rule of the Dutch. Anthony Colvé served as its governor and in the confused state of affairs had little time to prove whether he might be a good one or not. As it was, the townspeople probably remembered his elegant coach-and-four much longer than their owner.

Admiral Evertsen's conquest of New York had come a month too late for Holland, as news travelled across the ocean in those days. Peace was actually being declared in the Hague at the moment Captain Manning was surrendering the fort; Holland agreed to give up all captured territory, little dreaming that she was abandoning her only foothold in North America. Thus the pact was already sealed when word came that New York had been taken—all too late. "New Orange" was once more handed back to the Duke of York, who was not enthusiastic about receiving it; to him it had meant a great deal of trouble and disappointingly little revenue. He must have sighed as he appointed Edmund Andros as its new governor.

CHAPTER THIRTEEN

Windmills and Flour Barrels

B EAVER SKINS had gone a long way toward establishing New York as a commercial seaport, but when the province was handed back to the duke, something more was needed to increase the revenues from its trade. A few insignificant little taxes could never satisfy the duke's expensive tastes. Accordingly, the windmill and flour barrels made their appearance in the seal of New York City, commemorating the next important step taken by this child of Commerce.

The Bolting Act, passed by the governor and the council in 1680, gave to the little settlement on the edge of a savage continent the monopoly of bolting and exporting flour. This act, the first piece of business good fortune that had come its way since the day of the lowly beaver, had a wonderful effect on the city's growth, trebling its wealth and population in the next sixteen years.

Among the distinguished men attracted to the Hudson River region by its era of prosperity was Robert Livingston, who bought a great tract of land, including most of the present Dutchess and Columbia Counties, and established the home later known as Clermont. Here grew up a family destined for generations to take a prominent part in New York's affairs.

The revenues from the Bolting Act had already brought prosperity to the city, but those same revenues had a way of remaining in the pockets of the local merchants, to the bitter disappointment of the greedy duke. He began to think seriously of giving up his territory, but William Penn, at the moment negotiating for his own colony in America, advised him to grant the petition for colonial representation, and see if this would not produce a better spirit among the inhabitants.

The present seal of New York City.

The population of New York was now three thousand. It was the only colony denied a voice in its own government. Fortunately, Governor Andros appeared in England to clear himself from the suspicion of having kept out some of the profits, and no sooner had he re-instated himself in the good graces of Duke James, than he added his voice to that of Penn. The duke decided to follow their advice, and sent over Thomas Dongan as governor, armed with permission for the long-desired assembly.

The Assembly of the Province of New York, to which eighteen representatives were elected, drew up a "Charter of Liberties and Privileges" calling for self-government, self-taxation, a jury of twelve and other reforms. It was duly signed and sealed by the duke under date of October 30, 1683, but its delivery was put off. However, the colony went right on as if it had been granted, and much was gained—for a while.

Dongan divided the city into six wards, of which the town of Harlem was the sixth, and made the rest of the province into counties bearing their present names—Kings, Queens, Suffolk, Dutchess, Richmond, New York, Orange, Ulster, Albany, Westchester, Dukes and Cornwall. All creeds worshipped in the same church on Manhattan; the Dutch in the morning, the French at noon and the English in the afternoon. Since Andros' time, all the court records had been kept in the English language, and this, together with the free social life of the town, gave fresh encouragement to education.

In spite of constant troubles with the French and Indians along the Canadian border, which kept the colony in a state of unrest, much was done to improve the city. Wall Street was laid out on the site of the old fortifications, and public wells were dug. In 1686, Governor Dongan gave to New York a charter which forms the basis of real estate titles and wharfage rights of today. This document has been called the most liberal charter ever given a city, and under it, for the first time, New York was able to plan far-sightedly for a great development.

CHAPTER FOURTEEN

The Leisler Rebellion

SUDDENLY, all the growth and prosperity of the colony was threatened. On February 6, 1685, King Charles, sitting in the midst of his frivolous court, turned pale, sickened and died, leaving the Duke of York and Albany to carry on as James II. The way the new king chose to "carry on" had much to do with the unhappy conditions which followed in New York. He tore up the undelivered Charter of Liberties and Privileges, declared all other charters null and void, recalled Dongan and appointed Sir Edmund Andros to rule as royal governor over New York, New Jersey and New England, with Francis Nicholson as his lieutenant on Manhattan. Proud and aristocratic New York now found itself only a part of the general colonial system. With its seal broken and its assembly dissolved, with Huguenot tales of over-seas persecution filling the atmosphere with dread, New York felt itself on the eve of some dire calamity.

And calamity came. It took the form of "Leisler's Rebellion"—the result of rumor, confusion and fear. The imprudent James II had lasted on the throne of England only three years, when in 1688 he was overthrown and William and Mary of Orange were made rulers in his stead. Travelers brought vague news of this to the American colonies, but it was not confirmed for nearly a year, and in the meanwhile, there were so many rumors of plots and counter-plots that the populace became almost frenzied.

Governor-General Andros was deposed and thrown into prison in Boston, the capital of the combined colonies. This aroused the bolder spirits in New York to restlessness. They needed only a leader, and presently he appeared.

Jacob Leisler, a merchant of the city, was senior captain of the militia under Colonel Bayard, the collector of the port. He refused to pay duties on a cargo of wine, on the ground that the collector was a "papist." This act at once made him popular with the turbulent element. Bayard, together with the Schuylers, Van Cortlandts and Livingstons — all members of families which had received royal grants—was wrongly suspected of taking part in a plot to restore the detested James to the English throne. Excitement blazed when Leisler led a mutiny of the militia and seized the fort. Lieutenant-Governor Nicholson was arrested and foolishly permitted to sail for England, with his own side of the story prepared for royal ears.

It was now easy for Leisler to take control of the city, and he called an assembly that authorized him to act as dictator until a new governor

should be appointed by England. He, as well
as his son-in-law and lieutenant, Jacob Milbourne, undoubtedly felt that they were pro-
tecting New York from religious persecution.
Rumors that the Count de Frontenac was advancing from Canada to slaughter all the
Huguenots and subjugate the town, helped still
further to establish the temporary leadership of
these religious zealots. When the French and
Indians actually reached Schenectady, leaving
that unhappy village in ruins, Leisler called the
first Provincial Congress from seven colonies to
meet in New York and devise means for a common defense. The plans were hopelessly bun-
gled; an expedition which was sent against the
French failed because of mismanagement.

The aristocratic families of New York bitterly resented the rule of this son of the people.
As for Leisler, an unfortunate lack of balance,
and a vanity born of his new power, led him into
all sorts of indiscretions. He embarked on a
ruthless policy of throwing all who opposed him
into prison, pursued Van Cortlandt, Livingston
and Bayard with especial hatred, so that by the
time news of all this had reached William and
Mary, he had gone so far that death at the hands
of his enemies would have followed had he re-
laxed the vigor of his persecution.

The new sovereign had sent instructions addressed to Nicholson, or "such other person as

The Leisler Rebellion

The execution of Jacob Leisler echoed through the history of New York for years.

for the time being may be in authority," and Leisler naturally interpreted this to mean himself. In 1691 Colonel Henry Sloughter was appointed governor of the province. His lieutenant, Ingoldsby, unfortunately arrived in New York ahead of the new governor, with the intention of relieving Leisler, but with no official papers to prove his right. Leisler, therefore, refused to surrender the fort. Skirmishing went on, with some bloodshed, until Sloughter landed, at which time Leisler, professing to have awaited only the proof of the new governor's authority, surrendered.

His apologies and explanations came too late, however, to suit the temper of those he had persecuted, and after a trial, conviction and sentence that were pitifully swift as well as unjust, he and Milbourne were led out and hanged near the present site of the World Building.

The sobs and groans of the crowd that collected to watch this execution echoed through the history of New York for years in the bitterness of two parties thus formed—the Leislerians and the Anti-Leislerians. Even the sudden death of Governor Sloughter, which followed shortly after the hangings, was believed by many to have been due to a poison plot. This over-zealous captain of militia, who had been martyred for what he believed to be only patriotic service to his adopted country and to the new king, was vindicated later by Parliament, which restored his property and his good name to his heirs. Although this was done "as an act of their Majesties' mercy," it was in view of the fact that Leisler had not been guilty of treason.

The accession of William and Mary gave enfranchisement to the citizens of New York, although certain property qualifications kept the very poor from voting. Having gained so much, the keen merchants of New York entered straightway upon a long campaign for political supremacy, so that meetings of the assembly became a battle-ground for the control of funds.

CHAPTER FIFTEEN

Pieces of Eight

SO MUCH feeling had been aroused by the Leisler hanging that New York was more or less turbulent for years. It was a restless little city, full of the spirit of adventure, sometimes of violence. Many races jostled each other in the streets, and, as these same races were fighting in Europe, it was natural that they should quarrel here. Everything was new, the future uncertain, and the frequent changes of flag had been unsettling.

Governor Fletcher, who had succeeded Sloughter, was an Episcopalian, and under his encouragement Trinity Church was established where it now stands, on a corner of the old West India Company's bouwerie. During the construction, many prominent citizens made donations of their money or service. Among them, one Captain William Kidd, a highly esteemed merchant whose packet plied between New York and London, and whose comfortable home in Hanover Square boasted the first Turkish rug ever imported, lent his "runner and tackle" for the worthy cause.

Neither the political struggles between Governor Fletcher and the assembly over appropriations, nor the repeal by Parliament of the famous Bolting Act, which the citizens claimed would spell poverty and ruin, could stay the growing prosperity of the city. Some magic transformation was affecting its appearance. The little space New York then occupied below Wall Street began to fill up with fine new brick mansions of three or even four stories, containing such luxuries as heavy Spanish silver plate, carved ivories from the Orient, and odd fabrics from Madagascar. Men who traded over the seas began to wear more silver buttons and finer brocaded coats, and live like potentates.

Nor was this quite all. In and out of the taverns along the Strand swaggered bold-eyed men whose heavy earrings and long dirks, half-sheathed in a flaring boot or wide sash, must have seemed out of place in the drawing-rooms of Broadway and Wall Street, where, it is said, these pirates appeared. The Leislerian party, which had somehow succeeded in getting Robert Livingston to represent its interests in London, insisted on the recall of Governor Fletcher. Just how far he connived at the spread of piracy, was never established. It is known that he often entertained a notorious buccaneer named Tew at the executive mansion, and it was suspected that not all of Mrs. Fletcher's gems had gone through the "customs."

But for an incident quite unrelated to the governor, King William might not have taken

Under Governor Fletcher many New York merchants became pirates and hoisted the black flag.

action in the matter of piracy, for it was a practice that long years of sea-fighting had made fairly acceptable in good society. Some of the best people in New York were engaged in it. But it so happened that the treasure-ship of a powerful Indian rajah had been seized, so that it became urgent upon King William to make some demonstration against privateering. As there were no funds in Parliament for fitting up an offensive, Lord Bellomont, Robert Livingston and others suggested to the king that he should authorize a private undertaking, in which he should have a share of the profits when pirates were captured and their booty seized.

It sounded well, and at the recommendation of Bellomont and Livingston, the worthy Captain Kidd, whose "runner and tackle" were used in the building of Trinity Church, was selected. He was fitted out with a frigate, well-named the "Adventure," the king's seal and a nondescript crew of ninety men.

Lord Bellomont was appointed governor in place of Fletcher, and King William gave him instructions to stamp out piracy. Scarcely had his troubles begun when word reached New York that Captain Kidd, the supposed foe of the buccaneer, had himself hoisted the black flag and was now the terror of the seas! The stockholders of the "Adventure," from the king down, found themselves in a distressing predicament; there might be some rich dividends, but these were going to require much explanation, if the facts leaked out.

When this state of affairs had lasted much too long for royal comfort, King William issued a proclamation offering pardon to reformed pirates, but making a special exception in the case of "one William Kidd." Then suddenly Kidd appeared on Gardiner's Island, where much of his treasure was supposed to have been buried, and from there sent word to Bellomont asking for his protection. Bellomont assured him of this if he could explain his conduct, and the captain walked into the trap. The explanation was a story of mutiny on the part of the crew, in an effort to suppress which Kidd had struck down his mate. Bellomont clapped him in chains and sent him to London to stand trial.

To get him disposed of without involving his royal "backers" was the chief purpose of that farcical trial. In consequence, he was hurriedly hanged at Execution Dock on the first charge—that of having killed his mate. The charge of piracy was not gone into too deeply, for reasons which doubtless seemed adequate to the prosecutor representing the crown.

CHAPTER SIXTEEN

New York Wins Freedom of the Press

ABOUT a century had passed since Captain
Hudson sailed up the bay. Notwithstand-
ing its sturdy Dutch origin, English
speech and customs had established themselves
firmly in the infant city, and the voice of Anglo-
Saxon political freedom was beginning to sound
more distinctly through the rumble of commerce. For instance, when the profligate Governor Cornbury, who succeeded Bellomont,
misappropriated to his own uses a sum which the
assembly had voted for a better fortress at the
Narrows, the irate New Yorkers forgot, once
and for all, that they had been Leislerians and
anti-Leislerians and drew up a list of grievances
addressed to Queen Anne.

The new Governor Lovelace found the colonies had gained a major political point. From
now on, they voted revenues yearly and only for
a specific purpose. Abraham de Peyster served
as the first city treasurer, holding that office
for forty-six years.

Public funds in New York were at a low ebb,
but individual prosperity had reached a high
mark. A few white and gilded coaches, with
coats of arms emblazoned on their doors, rattled
over the tree-lined streets, and coffee houses

sprouted up here and there to lend a social atmosphere to merchandising. Queen Anne began to show her personal interest in the colony's problems by sending over, at her own expense, three thousand German refugees from the Palatine, who settled along the Hudson River and added 10 per cent. to the population of the province. The queen also made large grants to Trinity Church.

One of New York's worst problems was a racial one, for the huge number of slaves, imported earlier from Angola, had had little chance to emerge from savagery. In 1712, public nervousness over a plot to burn the city resulted in the death of forty negroes, who were hanged or tortured in the horrible fashion of the times.

Yet progress went on. Each new governor dispatched by the English "over-lords" three thousand miles away, found the little assembly more determined than ever to have its own way. Where other colonies had a majority of English citizens and lived in a world more restricted by agricultural pursuits and the difficulties of communication, New York, from the first, looked out through the eyes of many nationalities upon world affairs. Its assembly began to worry Parliament by its independence and arrogance.

When in 1720 Governor Burnet prohibited Albany from trading in Indian goods with

Canada, more wealth began to pour through the "market place" at the mouth of the Hudson River. In a few years, its commerce had outstripped that of Boston and Philadelphia, although these cities still claimed greater populations than New York.

Governor Fletcher had brought William Bradford from Pennsylvania in 1693 to open the first printing establishment in New York and, by the time William Cosby received his appointment as governor, Bradford had started the first newspaper, the "Weekly Gazette." As the result of a bitter quarrel between Cosby and an influential citizen, Rip Van Dam, a second newspaper, representing the Van Dam (or popular) faction came into being. Peter Zenger, one of the Palatine immigrants, edited this "Weekly Journal," and there was no doubt about the success of the new paper with the general public, for its witticisms, ballads and satires at the expense of the government, and especially of Cosby, were read with delight.

Zenger was presently thrown into prison by the enraged Cosby and his trial on the charge of libel not only stirred his fellow-townsmen, but echoed throughout the other colonies as well. Matters looked very black indeed for the poor little printer, but a dramatic surprise awaited the spectators in the crowded courtroom on the day of the trial. Andrew Hamilton of Philadelphia, then eighty years of age and the greatest lawyer in America, had offered himself eagerly as counsel for the defense.

"It is not the cause of a poor printer, nor of New York alone which you are now trying," he said. "No! It is the best cause; it is the cause of liberty, both of exposing and opposing arbitrary power by speaking and writing truth!" His arguments, delivered with an overwhelming eloquence that confused the prosecution, established beyond question the difference between libel and truth—the right of free speech. After only a few minutes of deliberation, the jury brought in a verdict of "Not Guilty!" and the triumphant shouts of the audience shook the courtroom. There was no controlling New York's exultation; all doors were thrown open to Hamilton; public dinners and balls were held in his honor and gifts were presented to him. The cannon which saluted the departure for Philadelphia of this champion of free speech introduced a new, stern, prophetic note into the voice destined to speak so soon for all the colonies in behalf of a still greater liberty.

CHAPTER SEVENTEEN

The Spirit of Liberty Grows

IN THE half-century between the ballads of
Zenger and the bullets of Lexington, the
drama of New York was a play of rapid
action, mounting toward an inevitable climax of
bloodshed. Through its various scenes still hurried rebellious slaves, threatening Indian war-
riors, French soldiery, public-spirited merchants
and swashbuckling pirates, fine ladies in coach-
and- six, and an ever-increasing number of keen-
eyed, defiant patriots. As the center of action
shifted from the British Parliament to the local
assembly, from Manhattan to Long Island, two
places became more and more the familiar background of speech and act. These were Bowling
Green and the Common, now known as City
Hall Park.

Since the days when the fort had been "New
Amsterdam," the open space before its walls
had variously served the public need. In turn,
it had harbored the gay booths of a Dutch fair,
echoed the angry shouts of a Leislerian mob,
and had smoothed itself out into a promenade
for the provincial belles and the handsome
young officers of the garrison.

By 1733, the mansions of the Verplancks, the
Livingstons and the Kennedys had given to the

spot a definite social tone, and in that year the council rented it to John Chambers, Peter Bayard and Peter Jay for one peppercorn per year, in return for which it was to be fenced about and maintained as a public bowling ground. So many stirring events took place on the Bowling Green that the history of the period preceding the Revolution might well be traced from them alone.

In the time of Stuyvesant, the Common was a public pasture for cows. To its open fields the town cowherd drove his charges up the trail that was to become Broadway, and at night a shrill blast from the horn that hung by every farmer's gate announced the herd's safe return. By 1775 the Bridewell Prison overlooked the Common, which had become a militia drill ground as well as a public meeting place.

But before that day New York had many throes to suffer. There were frequent epidemics of yellow fever; there were increased quarrels between the British Parliament, represented by the governors, and the assembly, representing the people. The chartering, in 1754, of King's College (now Columbia University) was one of the signs of the times. This institution, paid for by public lotteries, was founded, said Parliament: —"to prevent the growth of republican principles which already too much prevail in the colonies." Unfortunately for Parliament's in-

From the ranks of King's College came Alexander Hamilton with his artillery squad, to drill on the Common.

tention, the period of the American Revolution found the student ranks of King's College filled with eager young patriots—and from their number came Alexander Hamilton with his intrepid artillery squad to join the Sons of Liberty.

The winter of 1741 was an especially hard one, with the East River frozen solidly over so that teams could be driven across to Long Island. In February, an event occurred that was to plunge the city into a terrible tragedy. Robert Hogg, who lived on the corner of Broad and South William Streets was robbed. The theft was found to involve a low tavern keeper, his wife, and Mary Burton, their servant. While their case was pending, fires began to break out in different parts of the city. The governor's house in the fort was partially burned, and by the time nine of these fires had been discovered and checked, the public mind was thoroughly saturated with terror. The dread whisper of a negro plot went from lip to lip and the town quite lost its reason. A reward of one hundred pounds was offered, and Mary Burton began to remember amazing things. As fast as she implicated them, negroes were taken into custody, and in the hope of escaping a hideous death, these, too, began to throw the blame on others. Over a hundred of the poor wretches were imprisoned, hanged, or burned at the stake. Then Mary Burton got around to naming reputable people. The public was startled, and woke up from its nightmare, too late, however, for its innocent victims.

In the meanwhile, the English Parliament was losing patience with New York; privateering had become worse than ever during the long war with the French; the old Navigation Act was openly violated because it demanded that the colonies restrict their trade to English ports and vessels; and the prosperous merchants of New York steadily refused to vote generous sums for British officials to spend. The bold tone of their refusals was moreover beginning to echo in the other colonies.

British ministers looked at the luxurious homes of the stubborn merchants, especially at the Walton mansion in Pearl and Franklin Streets, and shook their heads. Something had to be done to make colonial possessions yield better dividends.

In 1762, the New York Assembly was given a choice: either it must vote an appropriation for the British troops stationed in the fort, or else it could pass no laws whatever. New York accepted the challenge, and for two years not a single measure was voted upon. That the New Yorkers were guided by a principle, and were really generous at heart, was proven again and again. For example, when the needy Methodists built their meeting house in John Street during this time, every creed united with them to help complete it. However, the assembly finally gave in, and voted the appropriation.

Then more alarming rumors began to drift across the Atlantic; it was said that Parliament planned a Stamp Act as a means of collecting taxes from her unwilling colonies. This possibility at once divided New York into two parties, the Tory Loyalists and the Whig Republicans. The latter formed the majority of the assembly at the moment, and a formal protest was sent to the king. At the same time, this party wrote to the other colonies and it was decided to call a Stamp Act Congress in New York.

John Cruger, Leonard Lispenard and William Bayard drew up a remonstrance, addressed to the British House of Commons.

In spite of all this vigorous protest, ships arrived in the harbor with the stamps. A group of impulsive young fire-brands had organized themselves into the Sons of Liberty, with Isaac Sears, John Lamb and Alexander McDougall at their head. They caused the bells to be tolled and flags put at half mast; they burned the effigy of Lieutenant-Governor Cadwallader Colden, and they intimidated General Gage, who was in charge of the fort, into giving up the stamps to the mayor, who promptly locked them up in the City Hall.

The next day, a group of merchants assembled in Burns' Coffee House and drew up a Non-Importation Agreement by which they bound themselves to boycott English goods, although this would be ruinous to their own fortunes. It was an act of unselfish patriotism. The merchants who met at Burns' Coffee House were highly respected citizens from the old, conservative families and their act stiffened resistance throughout the colonies. In addition to drawing up the agreement, they established a Committee of Correspondence with New England and Virginia. Because of their common cause, the colonies, under the leadership of New York, were beginning to think together as a nation.

While the stamps remained securely locked in the City Hall, and men began wearing homespun; while British ships guarded the harbor and prevented merchant vessels from trading, commerce came to a full stop. Then Pitt's eloquence spurred the British Parliament to repeal the obnoxious Stamp Act. This triumph deserved a celebration, and the New York Provincial Assembly erected a statue to George III in Bowling Green, while the Sons of Liberty, much to the chagrin of the garrison soldiers, set up a "liberty pole" on the Common.

CHAPTER EIGHTEEN

Golden Hill and Lexington

THE shouts of gratitude to King George had
scarcely died away in Bowling Green and
on the Common, when the wary merchant-
citizens discovered a fresh grievance. While the
Stamp Act had been repealed by the English
Government, an equally offensive Mutiny Act
had been passed, throwing upon New York the
full cost of the soldiers' upkeep. Indignation
flamed anew. Nor was this evidence of a fickle
spirit—the very steadfastness with which the
little city on the shore of a vast continent was
clinging to its standards of freedom had turned
gratitude into rage. King George's statue in
Bowling Green became a detested object and
the liberty pole on the Common a symbol of
the smoldering ill will between the populace and
the soldiers. Four times the Sons of Liberty
raised its wooden shaft, and four times the
soldiers cut it down.

Then, in 1767, Parliament passed the Townshend Acts, which deprived the New York Assembly of legislative power and imposed duties
on all imports. The assembly defied Parliament; it continued to meet.

The enterprising Samuel Fraunces had purchased Etienne de Lancey's fine mansion on the

southeast corner of Broad and Dock (Pearl) Streets in 1762, fitting it up as the Queen's Head Tavern, and now its great upper room became the scene of important public happenings. A group of the same harassed but determined merchants who had resisted the Stamp Act, met there in 1768 to form the first Chamber of Commerce with John Cruger as president. They numbered among them such sugar re-finers, ship chandlers and importers as Isaac Roosevelt, John Alsop, Isaac Low, members of the Ludlow family from Brooklyn Heights, the Baches, the Franklins, and the Schermerhorns. However, when these merchants voted to submit to all import duties except the tax on tea, the Sons of Liberty, who represented the working classes, protested vigor-ously against their action.

Fraunces' Tavern.

A first skirmish between the Sons of Liberty and the soldiers took place on August 11, 1766, but what has more justly been called the first "battle" of the Revolution, with bloodshed on both sides, occurred in New York in 1770. In that year, the British soldiers for the fifth time cut down the liberty pole and began tacking up taunting placards around the town. Isaac Sears and two others came upon some of the garrison at this work, and blows were exchanged. Presently twenty soldiers arrived on the scene; a mob of three thousand gathered and the storm broke. The townspeople, armed with knives and clubs, beat back the soldiers as far as Golden Hill (on John Street near Cliff) where the intervention of officers sent them back to the barracks and restored order.

A few years of comparative quiet followed, and though business was dull and poverty spreading, life in New York seemed to go on much as before the disturbances. Roger Morris had built the mansion, famous to this day as the Morris House or Jumel Mansion, and had wedded the beautiful Mary Phillipse, once courted in her father's home in Yonkers by Washington. The New York Hospital was erected by public subscription. In the Presbyterian "Brick Church" on Beekman Street, the celebrated Jonathan Edwards came to preach for a short time. The first milestones set up in the city were placed in 1769, measuring from the City Hall (at the corner of Wall and Nassau Streets) northward along the Bowery and Kingsbridge Roads. At the present 181st Street and Broadway, the famous Blue Bell Tavern opened its doors to weary travelers.

Suddenly the packets from London brought news that England meant to force her colonies to pay the tea tax. All the old slumbering resentment flamed high once more; the Sons of Liberty reorganized, and an assembly of citizens met and voted to send back any tea ships that arrived. The first one came just as the vessel bearing the unpopular Governor Tryon off for a holiday in England disappeared on the horizon, and Lieutenant-Governor Colden wrung his hands while the citizens ordered the tea ships to face about and depart, to the ac-

*The first bloodshed in the Revolution occurred in New York
when the townspeople beat back the soldiers
as far as Golden Hill.*

companiment of much defiant parading and firing of cannon.

Boston had held her "tea party" in the meanwhile, and when Parliament's act closing the Port of Boston in reprisal was made known in New York, sympathetic indignation went further than words. A committee of fifty-one, with Isaac Low as chairman, sent out a call for the first Continental Congress representing all the colonies to meet in Philadelphia.

Each delegate that passed through the city, en route to the momentous convention, was enthusiastically greeted, and John Jay of New York, one of the representatives chosen by the Fifty-one, drafted the Declaration of Rights which the Congress adopted.

The Committee of Fifty-one was continued as a Committee of Sixty, to keep watch over the threatened liberty of New York, and when the regular assembly, by a small majority, failed to sanction the Continental Congress, the Sixty took a private vote of the city and sent their own representatives to the second Continental Congress. The assembly had not represented the true temper of the people, and dissolved.

From this moment, exciting events followed one another rapidly. The seventeen-year-old King's College student, Alexander Hamilton, made a stirring speech on the Common in behalf of representation. On one quiet Sunday noon, a foam-covered horse clattered into Broadway from the Bowery, bringing a rider with news of the battle of Lexington. The Liberty Boys rushed at once to the City Hall, and seized six hundred muskets stored there for the militia. When British troops from the upper barracks were ordered a few days later to embark on board the "Asia," Colonel Marinus Willett hastened to be on hand with his comrades of the Sons of Liberty. In Broad Street, he himself stopped the front horses of their ammunition carts and drove off with the supplies, to the consternation of the British commander.

A provincial congress, called in New York by the Committee, was increased to one hundred, and a secret Commission of Safety was appointed, which functioned throughout the war, often making its headquarters at the old Christopher house now standing in Willow Brook, Staten Island.

A state of war was recognized by the Continental Congress, and George Washington was made Commander-in-Chief of the army, with orders to proceed to Boston. Over on Long Island, toryism was rife, and a force was sent to disarm the inhabitants. Not all of that territory was opposed to war, however, for Nathaniel Woodhull, of Mastic, was elected president of the provincial assembly which gave Washington a vociferous welcome as he passed through

*"Washington ordered the Declaration of Independence read
to the soldiers, drawn up in brigade formation
about the Common."*

New York. A cooler reception was accorded the returning Governor Tryon that same day, and he soon thought it prudent to retire to a frigate in the harbor.

After the defeat of the British in Boston, Washington made New York his headquarters, living at first in the de Peyster house in Pearl Street, opposite Cedar. It was then that his attention was called to a youthful artillery captain whom General Greene had watched drilling his men on the Common. This was Alexander Hamilton, destined to become Washington's most valuable aide at a later period of the war.

On the Fourth of July, 1776, the second Continental Congress completed the final draft of the Declaration of Independence. New York was in a frenzied state of preparation when a copy of that document arrived on the ninth, and Washington ordered it read to the soldiers, drawn up in brigade formation about the Common. The wildest enthusiasm followed; cries of joy, gun shots, caps, flags, filled the air, and mobs rushed forth to Bowling Green to tear down the leaden statue of King George, later melted into good American bullets.

Then, on the twenty-second day of August, Lord Howe landed his troops on Long Island and New York passed from an era of documents and speeches into the reality of war.

CHAPTER NINETEEN

New York and Nathan Hale

AS BOAT after boat disgorged its red-coats on the shores of Gravesend, at least the suspense of awaiting the blow was ended for New York. But there was small hope of holding the city against Howe's superior force.

The battle of Long Island was a crushing defeat to the American forces. At Jamaica Pass, on the Flatbush Road, and at the site of the Greenwood Cemetery, two divisions were surprised and overcome. A third division under General Stirling was stationed at the Cortelyou house, near a bridge crossing the Gowanus Creek (at about the junction of Tenth Street and Fifth Avenue in the Brooklyn of today) and when he discovered that the enemy hemmed him in on three sides, he faced about with three hundred Maryland troopers and made a desperate counter-attack. The little body was hacked to pieces and he himself was captured, but the act of bravery gave the main body of troops a chance to escape.

Their escape seemed only a temporary one, however. Crippled and disheartened, the little remnant lay cooped up on Brooklyn Heights facing complete annihilation at the hands of the British. Two thousand of their comrades had

Mrs. Murray's luncheon table looked much more inviting to General Howe than the pursuit of American soldiers.

been slaughtered and three of their best officers made captive. In the meanwhile, the leisurely Howe, within earshot of his victims, awaited a convenient moment to reach out and put a stop to the Revolution.

But the night of August 29 was darkened by a heavy fog and no unusual sounds penetrated it to alarm the British sentries. When the sun arose in the morning, great was their dismay, therefore, to find that Washington's entire force had melted from Brooklyn Heights. Brigade after brigade had been rowed silently across to Manhattan and safety.

On Manhattan, General Putnam and his force were stationed in the region of Fifteenth Street, but Howe's forces were able to get behind him by making a successful landing at Kip's Bay (near Thirty-fourth Street), utterly routing the militia there on guard. Again, the fate of the American army was hanging by a very slender thread. As Washington galloped among the fleeing Kip's Bay defenders, trying in vain to rally them, he was keenly aware how easily the English general could throw his line of red-coats across from the East to the Hudson River, trap Putnam's forces and end the war.

General Putnam was having the same thought, and had about given up the idea of marching his weary soldiers up the Blooming-dale Road in the broiling sunshine to meet Howe's superior force at the cross-road near Murray Hill. His two eager young aides, Alex-ander Hamilton, now nineteen, and Aaron Burr, twenty, were of another mind. Burr knew every inch of Manhattan, and offered to conduct the troops by shortcuts and bypaths to safety. Hamilton and his student artillery division marched in the rear, with plucky Sergeant Hoyt, who had been the last man to leave Brooklyn Heights, again in charge of the hindmost gun. They wound along dusty lanes and through woods west of Eighth Avenue, skirted the Mur-ray cornfield and met Washington at what is now Broadway and Forty-third Street, where the Paramount Theatre stands.

A scant half-mile away stretched the cool green lawn of the Murray house. General Howe had not been especially eager to fight Americans and when, on this hot noonday, Mrs. Murray invited him and his officers to stop for luncheon, the prospect was infinitely more entertaining. While he loitered gallantly at the table of his hostess, Hoyt's gun rumbled over the junction between Kingsbridge Road and the Bloomingdale Road, across the present Central Park and through McGowan's Pass to safety. By so narrow a margin did they escape that their pursuers reached the junction before they were fully out of sight.

The British now held the lower part of Manhattan Island, but the American forces still retained the upper end, and it was important that Washington should learn of Howe's plans. He called for a volunteer to enter the enemy territory, and a young captain named Nathan Hale offered to go. In the character of a schoolteacher, he made his way up through the Bronx, into Connecticut, over to Long Island and down to lower Manhattan and obtained the needed information. Then, almost within reach of the American lines, he was recognized and captured. The following morning, condemned as a spy, he was led out to be hanged at the British

"I only regret," replied Nathan Hale, "that I have but one life to give for my country!"

"Artillery Park," near the Dove Tavern—at almost the northwest corner of Third Avenue and Sixty-sixth Street.

"Fine death for a soldier!" his captors are said to have jeered. "I only regret," replied Nathan Hale, "that I have but one life to give for my country!"—words that have thrilled five generations of Americans.

CHAPTER TWENTY

British Capture New York

THE NEWS of Hale's execution reached Washington at about the same time that fires began raging in different parts of captured New York. The flames were soon beyond control, and presently fully one-fourth of the city lay in blackened ruins. Trinity Church burned to the ground, and St. Paul's was saved only by the courage of a few citizens who clambered to its roof and extinguished the embers as they fell from nearby buildings. Howe was convinced that the destruction was caused by patriot incendiaries, and permitted his soldiers to inflict shocking penalties upon those suspected of having had a hand in the plot. At the same time, he established a strict martial rule over the city.

In the meantime, Fort Washington was being erected at 183rd Street, and the British general sent a company of light infantry to attack the forces encamped in the woods of Harlem Heights. The attackers blew a scornful fox-hunt call on their bugles as they went into action against Major Leitch and his detachment, sent to guard the territory where Columbia University now stands. Colonel Knowlton was dispatched later by Washington to make a flank attack on the enemy, and although these two gallant officers fell in the battle, their men drove off the British and pursued them across a buckwheat field (now the site of Barnard College) mocking their over-confident hunting calls with good effect. The utterly vanquished English force retreated precipitately as far as 105th Street. News of the battle of Harlem Heights put the first real hope into the hearts of the Americans, and the first serious doubt into the hearts of the enemy.

When General Howe moved up and gave evidence of planning an attack, with the aid of his brother, Admiral Howe, in charge of the fleet, Washington left a force under General Magaw in the fort and retreated with the main army into Westchester. There was every reason to believe the fort could be held successfully, but the patriots had reckoned without suspicion of treachery. Careful plans of the fortification, indicating their weaknesses, were drawn up by Adjutant-General William Demont, who confessed in 1792 that he had committed this dastardly act. As soon as the information was placed in his hands, Howe abandoned an unsuccessful Westchester campaign against the main body of the American Army to swoop down upon Fort Washington in four columns of attack. The most important command was entrusted to Baron Von Knyphausen, the Hessian general.

A little outpost at Kingsbridge was taken first, and a peremptory order to surrender or suffer massacre without quarter was sent to Magaw. From the Jersey shore, Washington looked on helplessly while the little garrison struggled to defend itself against odds that he did not suspect. Word that Greene was planning to send aid from Fort Lee, across the Hudson, only reached Magaw after he had agreed to more favorable terms of surrender than those first offered by the British, and the last American stronghold on Manhattan fell into the possession of the enemy.

During the hours of spirited defense of that fortress, the first blood was shed by an American woman in the Revolutionary cause. Margaret Corbin had accompanied her husband from the time he enlisted as a gunner in the Pennsylvania militia, and stood by his side throughout the siege of the doomed fortress on Harlem Heights. When he fell, mortally wounded, she carried on in his stead, and surrender found her still by the gun, although one arm had been nearly severed at the shoulder by enemy grapeshot.

The fall of Fort Washington left over two thousand American soldiers in captivity, and New York became the British prison headquarters for the duration of the Revolution. An old sugar-house on Liberty Street was converted into the most notorious of dungeons—crowded, stifling in summer and wretchedly cold in winter—while in the Middle Dutch Church at Nassau and Cedar Streets, pews were ripped out to make room for thousands of ragged, half-starved wretches who lay so tightly packed together on the hard floor by night that when one moved, all moved.

The terrible prison-ship "Jersey" lay in Wallabout Bay and the unfortunates committed to its dreary hold learned to expect no mercy. By day they were permitted to crawl about the decks, if disease and starvation had left them sufficient strength, but by night they were herded into the filth and darkness below, and sentries who guarded the single narrow grating that admitted air to the hold often amused themselves by thrusting their bayonets between the bars at the struggling, gasping victims. Provost Cunningham's proud boast that he had caused the death of more Yankees than had any battle was probably no idle one, for no less than eleven thousand bodies are said to have been carried away in the death-carts that rumbled daily through the streets of New York, and the guard's morning call at the grating was "Rebels, turn out your dead!" The bodies were often dumped in shallow ditches along the Brooklyn shore, where each tide uncovered human bones. Only in recent years were these tenderly gathered up from the simple tomb originally erected by the Tammany

Society near the shore, to find a suitable resting place in the Martyr's Tomb at Fort Greene Park, where a monument rises to commemorate men who could have escaped their fate by taking up arms for the British, but who preferred to die.

While these unhappy sufferers were wasting away in the prisons of New York, a city of tents had grown up from the blackened ruins on the eastern side of Broadway. Long Island, disarmed first by the Americans, now found herself plundered by the British. Her citizens were forced to doff their hats to the officers, submit to raids of foraging parties, and utter no complaint when captured American officers were billeted in their homes. Colonel Ethan Allen, the hero of Ticonderoga, was at one time quartered in the Rapaelje home on New Lots Road, but when he stood on the roof and gave three loud, indiscreet cheers for the defeat of his captors at Bennington, the Rapaelje family lost its boarder. He was removed to the Provost prison and later released by an exchange of prisoners.

CHAPTER TWENTY-ONE

Washington Enters New York

THERE were some social gaieties in New York during the long winters of its occupation, but these were mostly confined to the British officers. Theatres had been established since 1732, when an English troupe had rented a building owned by Rip Van Dam on Maiden Lane and Pearl Street, in which to give two or three performances a week. The Hallam family came over in 1753, and built a theatre in Nassau Street. Another theatre, on John Street, first opened in 1767, served the young British officers stationed in New York during the Revolution as a place for amateur theatricals.

Life was not very gay for the average inhabitant, however. There was constant fear lest the Indians swoop down upon Manhattan, and while Washington fought no more engagements within the limits of New York, there were forays by his soldiers into Staten Island, and skirmishing in the region of Kingsbridge, which kept the British from being too effective in the territory surrounding the city.

By the time George III recognized the fact that his armies had been defeated, and peace terms were agreed upon, many changes had taken place in the city. Another devastating fire

*The British colors fell before the Yankee ingenuity
of John Van Arsdale.*

had swept through its streets, carrying away the last notable relics of its Dutch ancestry. With one more scene of the Revolutionary War to be played against its background, New York was ready for a new kind of experience.

The last scene was brief. On November 25, 1783, the victorious American forces, under General Knox, swept down from Harlem through the Bowery Lane and took possession of the city. Leaving his troops, and accompanied by citizens on horseback and afoot, General Knox then rode back to join Washington at the Bull's Head Tavern in the Bowery for a triumphal entry. With General Washington and his suite advancing eight abreast in that glorious procession, rode also Governor Clinton, Lieutenant-Governor Pierre Van Cortlandt and members of the council for the temporary government of the Southern District of New York.

The British had withdrawn to Staten Island at General Knox's approach, attemping one little parting pleasantry. Nailed to the top of a greased flagpole which stood at the north bastion of Fort George (our present Battery), the British colors fluttered impudently in the wind. But their joke was no more successful than their arms in the face of Yankee ingenuity, for John Van Arsdale, a sailor boy, made his way to the top by nailing cleats to the staff as he climbed, having the halyards tied around his waist, and then unfurled the Stars and Stripes over the American city of New York.

On December 4, General Washington gave a farewell dinner to his staff at Fraunces' Tavern, and departed to surrender his commission as General of the American Armies into the hands of the Continental Congress at Annapolis. Then the merchants of the city put away their ragged uniforms of military service and turned their thoughts once more to the exchange of commodities, to trade and barter.

New York, the child of Commerce, came back to its own.

CHAPTER TWENTY-TWO

The First Parade

I T WAS a great day for New York when the British troops departed. The misery and destruction of war lay behind, and just ahead lay great tasks and tremendous opportunities. Throughout the new America, the crisis was in a sense a commercial one. Of course this was a challenge to the city that has always buried its past and hurried eagerly into the future. New York had been preparing just the kind of statesmen the hour required.

Reconstruction was one of the first great problems. Thousands of British sympathizers fled to New Brunswick and Nova Scotia, from the disfranchisement and confiscation laws that had been passed at once by the New York legislature. It is said that these loyalists included fully nine-tenths of the inhabitants of Long Island and Staten Island. There was much rebuilding to do. A state government, already established, had to be made effective.

The city's new life brought political opportunities. For a long time the State Assembly under Governor George Clinton met here, and in 1784 Congress, with Richard Henry Lee as its president, selected New York for its meeting-place. Mayor James Duane at once offered the

City Hall, standing in Wall Street on a part of the present Sub-Treasury Building site and a part of Nassau Street, for a Federal Hall, and here the Congress met in January of the following year. Wall Street, once a place of fine residences and shaded gardens, now had reason to consider itself the most important business street of the nation.

Commerce returned. The "Empress of China" from New York was the first vessel to carry the American flag to Asia. Business was on the move. A General Society of Merchants and Tradesmen banded together, and by 1786 thirty trades were represented in its membership. The Bank of New York was established under the guidance of Alexander Hamilton. The old Chamber of Commerce applied for a renewal of its charter. Wall Street was beginning to be a power.

Opportunity took other forms as well, and King's College, for years used as a soldiers' hospital, became "Columbia." De Witt Clinton, the governor's nephew, who was passing through the city to enroll at Princeton, was persuaded to become the first student, and Reverend William Cochrane was appointed instructor.

Meanwhile, the nation's leaders realized that it was necessary to work out a sounder form of government. Business required it, and in 1786, a convention of colonial representatives was

summoned at Annapolis to deal with commercial problems. Hamilton went as a delegate
and helped to provide for another convention in
Philadelphia the following year, at which he
again represented New York. The final fruit
of this second gathering was the Constitution of
the United States.

Now began a hot debate between two parties:
the Federalists led by Hamilton and Madison,
and the Anti-Federalists, led by Clinton and
Burr. New York City was overwhelmingly
Federalist, which means that it favored the creation of a strong central government. This
would be important for commercial welfare.

On September 17, 1787, the Federal Convention, meeting in Philadelphia, completed its
work of drafting the Federal Constitution, and
its final revision was entrusted to another New
Yorker, Gouverneur Morris. Washington, as
presiding officer, sent a draft of it at once to the
Congress of the United States, sitting in New
York, which, in turn, sent it to the several states
for ratification. A New York State Convention
at Poughkeepsie debated long and earnestly before ratifying it in July, 1788. In the meanwhile, ten other states had signed on the dotted
line, and New York City, the stronghold of the
Federalist party, was fairly bursting at the delay. Fresh paint gleamed on its walls and fences,
and Major L'Enfant was remodeling the old

City Hall building into a dignified capitol, with
Doric columns, marble stairways, and a wide
balcony facing Broad Street—a building fit for
the first meeting place of Congress under the
new Federal Constitution. At the City Tavern
on Broadway and at Murray's Wharf distinguished visitors were coming and going almost daily, in anticipation of the great events
about to happen. Prosperity had come back to
New York, but material prosperity could not
satisfy the city with its ideals of government
hanging in the balance; it determined to force
action at Poughkeepsie.

Accordingly, on July 23, 1788, New York held
its first great parade. A committee of citizens
planned the various divisions of this procession,
which included over five thousand people and
stretched out for a mile and a half in length.
Every trade and profession, every age and class
represented in New York took part, appro-
priately costumed. Escorted by military bands,
there were divisions of marching clergymen,
Columbia students, judges, butchers, bakers,
brewers and candle-stick makers. Great floats
rolled by, demonstrating various mechanical
trades; a printing-press ran off the words of a
commemorative song which was distributed to
the crowds; coopers made barrels; and bakers
exhibited an achievement labeled "Federal
Loaf," marked in slices for the states. No man

was too important or too dignified to march that day. Noah Webster took his place among the publishing crafts, the Chamber of Commerce turned out in a body, and the last division was filled with gentlemen of no profession and by noted visitors and strangers. The great feature, however, was the huge "float," drawn by ten horses, representing the Federal ship "Hamilton" under full sail, which halted at Bowling Green and elsewhere on the route to fire a salute of thirteen guns from her deck. The procession was reviewed by the president and members of Congress at the fort. The "animated joy of the citizens of New York" was expressed along the line of progress through the crowded streets to the Bayard estate (near the present Grand Street) where tables had been laid beneath the trees for six thousand people.

In the time of strife and jealousy, New York rose as a unit, and spoke with power. Its voice carried to Poughkeepsie, and on the following Saturday, the State Convention ratified the Constitution of the United States. Then, on March 4, 1789, the new Congress began to assemble at Federal Hall. By April 6, there had been cast a unanimous electoral vote for George Washington as the first President of the United States.

CHAPTER TWENTY-THREE

Wall Street Becomes Famous

THE new New York—the free *American* New York—already had had two great days: November 25, 1783, when the British had evacuated the city, and July 23, 1788, when the mighty Federalist procession had proclaimed New York's support for the Constitution. Now it was about to have a third—a significant and joyous day—for a new government was preparing to take its place among the powers of the world, and the beloved Washington was on his way here to be inaugurated as its first President. Great were the preparations! Samuel Osgood's fine house at No. 3 Cherry Street (already used by the presidents of Congress) was redecorated for the Executive Mansion, and by April, a barge about fifty feet long had been constructed for the trip from Elizabethtown to Murray's Wharf at the foot of Wall Street, where carpeted stairs awaited the Presidential landing.

On April 23, all was aflutter! Balconies, housetops, docks, and all the little boats in the harbor were crowded by the eager multitude. As the canopied barge came into view around Staten Island, a salute of thirteen guns boomed from the Battery, flags were run to every masttop, and the waving hats of the crowd that cheered along the shore looked like a field of grain swayed by the wind. Thirteen white-clad pilots rowed the barge, with Commodore James Nicholson as commander and Captain Thomas Randall serving as coxswain, while at the landing-place a military escort surrounded the coach provided for General Washington's further progress. He chose, however, to walk through the flag-hung, crowded streets to his new home.

The week that followed was an exciting one indeed. What with gay illumination in every house, formal dinners and a ball or two keeping the city awake by night, a state election stirring all the rabid politicians on Tuesday and the Presidential inauguration to thrill the populace on Thursday, Friday must have found everyone nearly exhausted. With foreign ambassadors and curious visitors thronging the streets, all the new produce markets and little dry-goods shops and bookstores opening up in Hanover Square and along Pearl Street probably did a thriving business during those days.

Bright and early on the morning of April 30, the inauguration ceremonies began with services in all the churches. At twelve, a stately procession took its way to Cherry Street, that Washington, soberly dressed in brown homespun, might be escorted with all dignity to Federal Hall. Over its broad balcony a striped awning had been hung, and here the oath of office was

*The oath of office was administered to George Washington,
the first President of the United States, while
Wall Street looked on.*

administered by Chancellor Livingston, while Wall Street looked on, hushed to silence.

As soon as Washington had repeated the oath and kissed the Bible, Livingston waved his hat to the people on the street and exclaimed "Long live George Washington, President of the United States!" Three cheers were given, while Washington bowed and then reentered the Hall. The statue of Washington that adorns the steps of the Sub-Treasury Building, erected on the site of the old Federal Hall, commemorates this greatest moment in Wall Street's singular history. At the conclusion of the ceremony, a flag raised above the cupola of the Hall, gave the signal for a salute from the Battery; bells pealed and the people everywhere gave vent to their emotions in prolonged shouting.

From Federal Hall, the Presidential party walked to the services in St. Paul's Chapel (for Trinity was still in the process of rebuilding) and the remainder of the day was given over to rejoicing. In this dramatic way did the wooded "Manna-hatin" of Hudson, the wilderness trading post of Christiaensen and Block, the Dutch Nieuw Amsterdam of Peter Stuyvesant, the English New York of Lovelace, the New Orange of Anthony Colvé, the New York of Sloughter and his successors, the home of Captain Kidd, and the battlefield of Washington and Howe become the first seat of government of the new nation.

To some of the travelers who visited New York during the next ten months, it seemed as if the city had no other object than gaiety. The three hundred or so who made up its social register—the Jays and Knoxes, the Roosevelts, the Izards, the Livingstons and Ludlows—all the old aristocratic Dutch, Huguenot and English families who had intermarried since the town was young—did have a good time; and they were rather extravagant, too, with their swords and powdered wigs, their satin waistcoats, knee buckles and silk stockings. The New York ladies of fashion, with their high, pomaded head-dresses and flaring hoops, demanded and enjoyed luxuries that equalled any to be found in the capitals of Europe.

The President and Mrs. Washington held formal levees twice each week, at which full dress was worn. The canary-colored presidential coach, adorned with cupids holding garlands of flowers, and drawn by six white horses stepping high on their painted hoofs, became an accustomed sight on the "fourteen-miles-round." This was the fashionable afternoon drive of the period. The route led up the old Boston Post Road (on the line of Third Avenue), crossed Murray Hill where Lexington Avenue now stretches, proceeded west through McGowan's Pass to Bloomingdale, and turned back to follow the Hudson River through Greenwich Village, and across Lispenard Meadows or through Love Lane (Twenty-first Street) into Broadway.

Into the Macomb house at No. 39 Broadway, Washington moved on his birthday, in 1790, with his family, his servants and secretaries. Old dilapidated Fort George, at the foot of Broadway, was torn down, and a government mansion was nearly completed on its site, when Congress decided to make Philadelphia the nation's capital instead of New York.

New York hesitated to cede jurisdiction over the ten square miles of territory that Congress demanded, and quite positively refused to give up its port taxes to the support of a resident Federal Government.

Once again Commerce decided the destiny of her favorite city.

CHAPTER TWENTY-FOUR

The Nation's Capital

IN October, 1789, before the change in the nation's capital had been decided, Washington made a tour of Long Island, visiting Flatbush, New Utrecht, Gravesend and Jamaica. He breakfasted with Henry Onderdonck in what is now the town of Roslyn, and dined in Flushing, where he was interested in the fine gardens of its inhabitants. He returned to Manhattan by way of Morrisania, in Westchester County, where lived Gouverneur Morris and his family.

At the time, Brooklyn Heights was being considered as a possible site for the federal capital, and while on this tour Washington also viewed that district of orchards and fine old homes. Pierrepont's Distillery stood then on Joralemon Street, and when his farm was later cut up into lots, he gave to the thoroughfares names of his old neighbors, like the Remsens. The town of Brooklyn was then little more than Fulton and Main Streets, with a row of stately elms leading from Orange to Clinton Street.

New York was distinguished not only because national headquarters were established here, but also because many of its citizens had won high posts of responsibility in the new government.

Gouverneur Morris, for example, was sent as envoy to France; Alexander Hamilton, as Secretary of the Treasury, was directing all his superhuman energies to the founding of a national bank, the funding of debts, and the establishment of a sound credit for our nation abroad. John Jay had been made the first Chief Justice and Samuel Osgood the first Postmaster-General under the new Constitution. Undoubtedly the most serious problems before the earnest little group of legislators gathered in Federal Hall during those ten experimental months were ones of finance and commercial relationships between states and with foreign nations. No men were so able to advise in these matters as the men bred in New York. In spite of the opposition of Jefferson and other strong Anti-Federalists, Hamilton's ideas about national banking and finance finally prevailed.

Back in 1780, officers of the Revolutionary Army had formed the Society of the Cincinnati. Later another organization known as the Tammany Society or Columbian Order, was started in New York by the "Sons of St. Tammany" (named for Tammenand, a Delaware brave) with the intention of offsetting the aristocratic tendencies of the former. Its first recorded meeting was held in the tavern of Talmadge Hall in Cortlandt Street as early as May 1, 1767. "This national institution," its

*The Nation's first Congress assembled at Federal
Hall in Wall Street.*

founders announced when it was revived in 1789, "holds up as its object the smile of charity, the chain of friendship, and the flame of liberty, and in general whatever may tend to perpetuate the love of freedom or the political advantage of this country."

New York gained much from its ten months' experience as the national as well as the state capital. More than ever before, and certainly in a more brilliant array, all races had journeyed up and down its streets. The formality and frequency of social affairs had stimulated a desire for culture, for languages, music and all the arts. Directly out of this stimulation was eventually developed New York's wonderful school system. One other great agency of education, the New York newspaper, owes its present supremacy to the stimulation it received in those days when Federalists and Anti-Federalists needed plenty of ink, space and all Noah Webster's listed words to express their contempt for each other.

In 1789, nine newspapers were hawked about the streets and read eagerly in the taverns and drawing-rooms. Among these, Sam Loudon's "Packet" appeared three times weekly; the "New York Journal" on Thursday; the "Daily Advertiser" rivalled the "Gazette" each day; while the "Gazette of the United States" came out on Wednesdays and Saturdays. Noah Web-

ster had established the first magazine, the
"American," in 1788, but its life had been a short
one. "The Minerva," his next and quite successful venture, became the ablest Federalist spokesman in the country.

Among the gay winter customs that delighted
the prosperous inhabitants of New York while
it was still the federal capital, were skating on
the Collect, sleighing parties into the country,
and brilliant cotillions where syllabub and float-
ing island refreshed the dancers. One old Dutch
habit pleased Washington best: "The highly-
favored situation of New York will in the
process of years attract numerous emigrants
who will gradually change its ancient customs
and manners," he observed, "but whatever
changes take place, never forget the cordial and
cheerful observance of New Year's Day."

At the little theatre in John Street he was
three times a visitor while in New York as
President. It was there, during a performance
of "Darby's Return," that he caused a minor sen-
sation by laughing—the only occasion of its kind
on record! His patronage and evident approval
meant much to the actors at a time when many
persons frowned upon the theatre as ungodly.

During the hot summer days of July and
August, 1790, Washington was host to the Creek
Indians who came to New York under their
sachem, Colonel Alexander McGillivray,

decked out in their blankets and feathers, to make a new peace treaty with Congress. The signing of that treaty was Washington's last act in the Wall Street Federal Hall. His full-length portrait had just been completed by Trumbull, and the Indians touched its cold surface with curiosity and astonishment.

Their visit was the last exciting event of New York's life as a national capital. Stage-coaches and elegant private carriages began to carry away the personal trappings of government leaders, and Washington went slowly down the steps of Murray's Wharf, took his position again in the red-curtained barge which had borne him to the city in such triumph ten months before, and turned to wave a reluctant farewell to its regretful townspeople. Mrs. Adams, the Vice-President's wife, wrote at length of their new home in Philadelphia, and of the arrangements for their convenience there: "When all is done," she mourned, "it will not be Broadway."

CHAPTER TWENTY-FIVE

The First Stock Exchange

IT WOULD not have been like Broadway to nurse its loneliness for more than one brief winter after the gay capital had flown elsewhere. Nor did Wall Street let go of its new-found importance, for Congress already had authorized the sale of $80,000,000 in bonds, and people were beginning to get their savings out of the cracked teapots for better investments. The whole country was awake, and New York was ready for the day's opportunity.

At about 68 Wall Street there stood, in 1790, a spreading buttonwood tree. Under its branches a dozen merchants began to congregate each day for the buying and selling of the new securities. This was the first Stock Exchange. By 1792, its membership had grown to twenty-four, with definite agreements about trading drawn up between them. On the corner of Broad and Wall Streets, John Broome, Gulian Verplanck, William Laight, and a few other prominent merchants gathered to form the Tontine Association, a novel kind of loan society, and the building they presently erected as the Tontine Coffee House, valued at $35,000, was the most costly mansion of the period in New York. It soon became the favorite meeting place for traders, and much

Under a buttonwood tree on Wall Street New York merchants gathered each day and established the first Stock Exchange.

history was made within those walls before it was destroyed by fire in 1804.

But war clouds had been gathering in Europe, and before long France was not only in the throes of her Revolution, but fighting England as well. This excitement was reflected in New York, so full of French sympathizers, and with the memories of the Wallabout prison ships still fresh. It was hard to be neutral. In resentment, England began to discriminate against American shipping, to the distress of New York merchants. Finally, Washington sent John Jay on a peace mission to Great Britain, and the result was his famous commercial treaty.

Just at this time, New York State elected John Jay as governor, and when he returned from London he was enthusiastically installed in the Government House on Bowling Green. The ceremonies were barely over when the terms of his treaty were made public. It looked like a betrayal of the French, and New York was furious. An angry mob collected in Wall Street, and when Rufus King and Alexander Hamilton tried to speak on behalf of the treaty, they were stoned. The crowd surged down to Bowling Green where a copy of the offending document was burned before the Government House. At the same time, however, the merchants forming the Chamber of Commerce quietly collected, assured themselves that the treaty provided the first real freedom American commerce had known on the high seas, and voted sixty to ten in its favor. Their vision was clear and accurate, for the Jay treaty was in reality a turning point for New York as an important port among world cities.

Ship-building began at once. In another five years, when the population had about doubled, the Rapaelje farm at Wallabout had become the Brooklyn Navy Yard; and the inventive genius of such men as John Fitch, John Stevens, Nicholas Roosevelt and Robert Livingston was already at work upon the problem of steam navigation. There was a movement to drain off the Collect Pond by making a wide ditch through Canal Street, but before this had been done, John Fitch, in 1796, had a chance to try out on its quiet waters his little vessel equipped with a ten-gallon iron pot as a boiler. Robert Livingston watched it make six miles an hour under its own steam, and persuaded the State Legislature to give him a twenty-year monopoly on this new form of navigation. Inventive genius had been given a sharp stimulus and by the time the little boat of John Fitch was declared impracticable, still another idea was taking form in the brain of Robert Fulton.

CHAPTER TWENTY-SIX

The First Public Utility

IN 1798, the same year that Albany became the state capital, a fearful epidemic of fever swept over New York City, carrying off hundreds upon hundreds of its inhabitants. All business was suspended; people fled to Greenwich Village and to Chelsea in hordes. The site of Washington Square was made a potters' field, and members of the Medical Society, formed some years earlier, served day and night to check the scourge. When it had again died down, New York set about profiting from the experience.

The New York Hospital had been founded in 1776, but had merely served as a barracks for soldiers until after the war. Since that time, physicians had been hampered in their work by popular superstition. On one occasion, a prying urchin had climbed a ladder to watch some doctors busily dissecting a corpse, and when one of them playfully brandished a limb to shoo off the boy, he hurried to broadcast a rumor that graves were being robbed. The result was the so-called "doctors riot," in which property was destroyed and the doctors' lives threatened.

New York, however, was ready to cooperate with science to stamp out yellow fever. Organization in charity work began to show itself, and the much-neglected matter of sanitation and a pure water supply became the question of the day. The city had been getting its water from wells and springs on Manhattan, and most of them were impure and brackish in taste. The most popular spring, the Tea Water, was in the vicinity of Baxter and Mulberry Streets, where a fashionable out-of-town garden resort was located. Water from this spring was peddled about the town in "Tea Water Carts" at three pence for 130 gallons. For a while, a spring at 8 Jacob Street rivalled it, claiming popularity from its "medicinal" character, and an elegant Moorish building was erected over the pump. This popularity ended, however, when somebody discovered that its peculiar taste came from a neighboring tan-pit!

The demand for a better water supply led to the formation of the Manhattan Company, New York's first public utility corporation. In 1799 the state legislature granted a charter authorizing a group of prominent citizens to supply the city with "pure and wholesome water." Among them was John Stevens, the famous engineer whose ambitious plans for a railroad later matured into the Pennsylvania System. Even the city itself was among the founders, for it became one of the first subscribers to the stock of the Manhattan Company and for over a

The Manhattan Company erected a reservoir on Chambers Street and laid its pine log pipes.

century was represented on the company's board of directors. A few years later, in 1808, the State of New York also became a stockholder and has since held its shares continuously for the benefit of the common school fund.

Aaron Burr, a member of the State Assembly from New York City in 1799, saw in the chartering of the water company an opportunity to gain banking privileges for his political party, the Anti-Federalists. Hitherto, all efforts on their part to get a bank charter past the legislature had been blocked by Alexander Hamilton and the Federalists, who meant to keep their monopoly in New York City.

Accordingly, Burr wrote a clause into the water company's charter, authorizing its directors to employ their surplus capital in any manner not contrary to the state and national laws. It was not until after the bill had been passed by the legislature and signed by the governor that Hamilton and his party realized that they had been outwitted. New York City now had three banks, the Bank of New York, a branch of the Bank of the United States, and the Bank of the Manhattan Company, known today as the Bank of Manhattan Trust Company.

Burr, for his part, derived small advantage from his manœuvre. It was not long before he was dropped from his seat on the directors' board of the Manhattan Company, defeated for re-election to the State Assembly, and kept by a single electoral vote from becoming President of the United States. Embittered by these defeats, he recognized Alexander Hamilton as their author, and in 1804 he challenged his rival to a duel at Weehawken. The shot that killed Alexander Hamilton ended two singular careers so bound up in the history of New York, for by the death of his adversary, Aaron Burr made himself an outcast from society.

CHAPTER TWENTY-SEVEN

Fulton's Steamboat

AT THE turn of the century, New York was dreaming already of its destiny. It had only about sixty thousand inhabitants, less than 1 per cent. of its present figure, and slightly less than Boston and Philadelphia, but the figure must have seemed impressive. Besides, New York had climbed to leadership in commerce.

Around the name of De Witt Clinton, for a long period mayor, and later state governor, much of the city's progress for the first quarter century is clustered. He, as well as Jedediah Peck, worked diligently toward the founding of a free public school system; he helped to form the New York Historical Society and promoted the establishment of an American Academy of Art. While music and art did not flourish in New York until after the Civil War—the first foreign violinist to plan concerts here advertised for work as a chimney-sweep the following year!—the encouragement during Clinton's time built the foundations.

Imagination was leading the way. In literature, the city's first real voice spoke through Washington Irving. His burlesque "Knickerbocker's History of New York" immediately set the whole country laughing at its absurd account of the old Dutch town, and still survives to give the name "Father Knickerbocker" to New York City as well as the name "knickers" to the golf costume of its inhabitants.

In 1807, imagination gave birth to a steamboat that actually navigated. It is true that Fitch's little steamer had shown that it could move on the Collect Pond, but churning around on this little patch of water could hardly be considered navigation. Now, Fulton with his "Clermont" really navigated. One of the most exciting days New York has ever known was August 17, 1807. An odd little craft with a

Fulton's "Clermont" started its historic trip up the Hudson River

smoke-stack and paddle wheels was about to start for Albany by the power of steam—a great and prophetic adventure. People hurried to the Greenwich Village dock. Sure enough, there she lay with smoke pouring from her funnel. Then, to the wild cheering of the crowd, she started up-stream along the course that Hudson had followed almost exactly two hundred years before. The era of steam navigation had begun! Most of the sail-boat owners muttered against the new invention, but Cornelius Vanderbilt, who had been sailing his little market boat daily between Staten Island and Manhattan, and saving up the pennies, joined forces with steam. It was not chance, but energy and foresight that won him first place in the shipping world.

Once more imagination and optimism scored in the little city on the lower end of Manhattan Island. In those days one began to get into the country at Chambers Street. The rear walls of the new City Hall were being faced with brown-stone instead of marble in the interest of economy; but the city planning commission proceeded to lay out the streets clear to 155th Street with longitudinal avenues, numbered cross streets, and extra wide streets at intervals—like Fourteenth, Twenty-third, Thirty-fourth, etc.—as if they were providing for a population of two millions! Great was the ridicule caused by this ambitious plan at the time—but the commission had been imbued with the imagination and daring that made the city. New York has always believed in the future. Even so, its faith was about to be tried, for just ahead lay three death blows to commerce—the "Embargo Act," the "Non-Intercourse Act," and the War of 1812.

CHAPTER TWENTY-EIGHT

"Don't Give up the Ship!"

WAR was just about the last thing New York wanted. However, during the first year some of the city merchants thought they saw a silver lining in the war-cloud, as they fitted out ship after ship for another era of privateering. The dividends were high.

New York's streets were not, at the very first, the scene of much excitement, for the British point of attack was elsewhere, and even the naval battles were fought beyond the horizon. But when Captain James Lawrence arrived in the "Constitution," fresh from his capture of the "Resolution," the city arose to give a glamorous welcome to the heroes. Gifts, dinners, salutes and enthusiastic cheers were the tribute to him and to each succeeding warrior guest.

Nor was Captain Lawrence unworthy of the city's acclaim. After more daring exploits in the "Constitution" and the "Hornet," he was placed in command of the "Chesapeake." Just off Halifax he encountered the British frigate "Shannon" and the two vessels closed with each other. It was a desperate fight. The anchor of Lawrence's ship caught in the hull of his foe in such a way as to render the guns of the "Chesapeake" useless and British shells at once raked her decks. As Captain Lawrence was carried below, mortally wounded, his last command, "Don't give up the ship!" held the sailors at their posts until the little vessel was completely overpowered. Later, in Trinity churchyard, the bodies of Captain Lawrence and his lieutenant, Augustus Ludlow, were both given a fitting heroes' burial.

The profits of war to ship-owning merchants ceased almost as abruptly as they had mounted. By the end of 1813, the British had thrown a blockade around New York harbor, bottling up all commerce as tightly as possible. The City of Washington was next invaded and sacked, and what there was of local indifference gave way to an immense activity. All selfish thought of personal gain was abandoned and when Mayor Clinton called a mass meeting for defense plans on August 10, 1814, the city arose again in supreme unity of purpose.

Nicholas Fish was made chairman of the Defense Committee, and met daily with De Witt Clinton and Henry Rutgers in the new City Hall. "Sooner let us die in the last ditch," he told the people in a stirring speech of exhortation, "than tamely and cowardly surrender this delightful city into the hands of an invading foe." Matters no longer stood as in 1664!

When the members of every society and trade gathered during those summer days and nights following the fall of Washington, there was no mere parade afoot this time. Each man came with pick-axe, shovel or wheelbarrow to build forts and entrenchments, and the defense of Brooklyn meant as much to Manhattan as the erection of barriers on Washington Heights concerned the men of Brooklyn. The moon was full, and the "Moonrise Workers" took up the spades where the "Sunrise Workers" dropped them. Tammany Society, the Sons of Erin, the Marine Society and many other lodges, each under its own leaders, alternated with plumbers, curriers, tanners, medical students and the entire enrollment of Columbia College in carrying on the work of defense. By a strange coincidence, the Columbia group, marching from their buildings at University Place, were assigned to the defenses at 123rd Street, practically upon the future site of their own campus. The spirit of cooperation spread, and one day men from Newark appeared, ready to help, carrying a sign "Don't give up the soil!"—evidently inspired by Lawrence's last words.

With such security, schools were soon reopened, and the volunteer ditch-diggers went back to their neglected shops. Barriers had been placed across Manhattan's upper end, the remains of which are standing today in Central Park at 110th Street, and at 123rd Street and Amsterdam Avenue. Brooklyn Heights fairly bristled with defenses. The newly built Castle William frowned over a prepared New York.

During all this, the British kept a close watch on the harbor, but Admiral Decatur slipped by one night and landed on Gardiner's Island, aided by Lion Gardiner, a descendant of its original manor-lord. The English heard a rumor of the event and swooped down for reprisals. Mrs. Gardiner was much too quick-witted for them, however. She put her husband to bed behind green curtains that gave his face a sickly pallor, strewed medicine bottles about, and met the invaders with such a convincing air of anxiety over her suffering patient, that the English officers tiptoed away without making any arrest.

However, the expected attack upon New York never occurred, and finally, in February, 1816, news came that a treaty of peace had been signed in Ghent. The frenzied celebration that took place marked the beginning of Modern New York.

CHAPTER TWENTY-NINE

The "Big Ditch" Opened

PROSPERITY fairly stumbled on the heels of the peace treaty. The commerce of the world had been thrown suddenly open to merchants of New York and they could scarcely wait to touch again the long-denied foreign "commodities." "We must have ships—more ships! and swift ones!" they cried.

By 1817 a little group of Quakers had established the first American line of packet ships, the Black Ball Line, sailing between New York and Liverpool. The Red Star came next in 1821, and long before the close of two decades when New York had grown to a metropolis of 165,000 population, there were three shipyards giving work to an army of builders and more packet lines opened, operating to pile up wealth for the ship-owners. Those were the bold and picturesque days when captains scorned the aid of tugs, and prided themselves upon their skill in entering or leaving the harbor.

In the meantime, the development of steam navigation had been hampered by the monopoly granted to Livingston. Once this was removed, in 1824, the Hudson River and the Sound echoed with the shrill blasts from steamboats. Fulton's steam frigate, the "Demologos," had been launched in 1814, equipped for discharging hot water onto enemy decks, and both Cornelius Vanderbilt and John Jacob Astor were ready to enter the steam-packet trade on the Hudson and the Atlantic.

In 1819, the "Savannah," the first American-built ocean-going steamship, was despatched from New York to Liverpool, but the experiment was not encouraging. Her machinery took up so much room that the cargo was crowded out, and off the coast of Ireland, she was pursued two days by a revenue cutter, whose captain was convinced that she must be on fire. For many years sailing vessels were to be the important vehicles of commerce.

For a long period, De Witt Clinton, without salary, had worked in the face of ridicule and opposition to make the Erie Canal a reality. "Clinton's Big Ditch," his enemies called it, but only while the project looked doubtful. In 1825, it was completed—a successful feat of engineering that was destined to enrich New York. While the city had been developing its foreign commerce, a vast continent had been opening up behind it. Explorers, traders and pioneers had been ascending rivers, opening clearings in the forests and planting settlements. After the woodmen had come the farmers, and now at many points there was a growing population requiring goods that still had to be imported from Europe.

*New York celebrated the opening
of the Erie Canal.*

The Canal had joined New York and the
awakening frontier.

In spite of its excellent harbor, New York
would never have grown without the Hudson
River. Along its stream the canoe, the sailboat
and the steamship, in turn, had hurried to dis-
tribute merchandise unloaded by ocean-going
vessels upon the city's wharves. Now, suddenly,
the territory served in this manner had grown
prodigiously. By one brilliant stroke, that trade
"hinterland" added to itself millions upon millions of acres in the Great Lakes region.

At ten o'clock on the morning of October 28, 1825, a cannon shot relayed the news to watchers along the Hudson that official canal-boats were on their way to Sandy Hook, and for nine days impatience mounted to fever height. Then New York went out in a vast, resplendent flotilla to welcome the "Seneca Chief" bearing De Witt Clinton and his party down the Hudson. The naval procession, greeted by music, gun salutes and much display of bright-colored flags, went around the Battery, touched at the Brooklyn Navy Yard, passed Castle William, and anchored beyond Sandy Hook, where Clinton emptied a keg of Erie water into the Atlantic as a symbol of the day's great significance. A land parade four miles and a half in length carried the festivities into the afternoon, and the evening was made gay by a huge ball in the Lafayette Theatre on West Broadway, then known as Laurens Street.

While the "Big Ditch" was still in the digging, in 1822, another fearful epidemic of yellow fever visited Manhattan Island. This time the generally filthy condition of the streets was blamed. Pigs had long been permitted to roam about as scavengers, in spite of protests from indignant ladies, crowded off the narrow sidewalks, and the complaints of peevish gentlemen who looked down over high choker collars and flowered stocks to find mud splattered on delicate fawn-colored trouser legs. Cleanliness was not regarded as indispensable; even bathtubs were rented rather than owned. Thus, in spite of the Manhattan Company's continuance of a water supply that brought it no profits, the fever took a heavy toll of lives. A high fence was built in 1822 in the region of Rector Street, enclosing both Grace and Trinity Churches, as a quarantine. Banks, business houses, the Custom House and Post Office moved almost overnight to Greenwich. An open field, now Bryant Park, was set aside for a public burial-ground and interments were discontinued in the place now known as Washington Square.

In the meantime, a record-breaking immigration, wave on wave, was causing over-population and an increase in pauperism and crime. The way in which New York met these problems by organization of charity set it apart from all other cities of the period. The same efficient, executive spirit that fashioned a sort of game out of money-making showed itself in the management of benefactions. In 1819, John Pintard and his associates established the Bank for Savings, the first in the city. Bellevue had long had a fever hospital as part of the institution formed from the Lindley Murray, Livingston and Kip estates on the East River. A public institution for the Instruction of the Deaf and Dumb was incorporated in 1817 and this step was followed

in 1818 by the laying of the corner stone of the
Bloomingdale Hospital for the Insane. Through
the hard winter of 1816-17, when an ice-bridge
formed over the East River so that hundreds of
people walked to Long Island, municipal soup
kitchens gave aid to the poor. The Society for
the Manumission of Slaves had been given a
good start by John Jay and other benevolent
citizens like Moses Rogers, whose home still
stands at 7 State Street. One significant reflection of public sentiment was a bill which Governor Tompkins signed in 1817 to free all slaves
by July 4, 1827, in New York State.

All, however, was not distress and poverty.
Alexander T. Stewart, one of New York's great
merchants, built a large store at 283 Broadway
for the sale of "fresh and seasonable dry goods"
—so far up-town that people shook their heads
over his folly. Twenty years later, he built the
marble "emporium" that still stands on the opposite side of Broadway between Chambers and
Reade Streets. A company began to supply New
York with that strange form of lighting known
as "illuminating gas." The Federal government
ceded Castle Clinton to the city and the great
building was remodeled into "Castle Garden,"
where one might dance with the mayor's permission but not play billiards!

This vast public auditorium was to witness
many brilliant scenes before giving place to the

Aquarium of today. In 1824, a reception was held there for the aged Lafayette, who was revisiting the country he had served as General Washington's aide. His visit was one of the most notable of New York's public welcomes.

Inspired by the high emotions of the moment, officers of the Eleventh Infantry Regiment met at the Shakespeare Tavern on the northwest corner of Nassau and Fulton Streets, and there formed the National Guard—later so famous as the Seventh Regiment of New York City. Everywhere there was enthusiasm, gaiety, evidence of prosperity. Citizens in gala attire thronged to pay their respects to the gallant old marquis, who was bewildered by this apparent equality in rank and wealth. "But where are the *people?*" he asked.

CHAPTER THIRTY

The Great Fire of '35

WITH the opening of the Erie Canal, New York seemed to realize that it was destined to become a giant, and began to reach out in every direction. By 1828, the Delaware and Hudson Canal gave it access to the rich coal fields of Pennsylvania. In 1832, ground was broken for the New York and Harlem Railroad. The first horse-cars travelled from Prince to Fourteenth Street in that year, and five years later their tracks reached to Harlem. The first railroad station arose where the Municipal Building now stands, and about the same time, the New York and Erie Railroad was incorporated and its construction begun.

The city was full of the spirit of scientific experiment. S. F. B. Morse, a professor in the recently formed University of the City of New York, situated on the east side of Washington Square, brought out, in 1837, a practical electric telegraph and transmission code. Submarine devices, life preservers, an apparatus for raising sunken ships, and, most important of all, steam locomotives, were variously exhibited to capitalists eager for investments. New York, with its wealth, its adventurous spirit and its tremendous energy, became the natural place to or-

ganize enterprises. It was growing at a phe-
nomenal rate and contained more people than
Baltimore, Philadelphia and Boston, its closest
rivals, combined. Gulian Verplanck, an old
New Yorker, re-
marked that his na-
tive city had become
a "sort of thorough-
fare where almost
every remarkable
character is seen
once in the course of
his life."

Morse improved telegraphy.

However, the year
1834, in which Brooklyn was incorporated as a
full-fledged city, was not a happy one in New
York. There were hard times again, with a
gradual rise in rents and prices. Considerable
ill-concealed bad feeling existed among the
mixed races that were giving the "Five Points"
region on the Bowery an unsavory reputation,
and this feeling was constantly flaring up in the
form of riots which the city militia was called
upon to quell.

Newspapers, delivered by messenger, were
expensive, and contained mostly political
speeches, advertisements and shipping news.
Horace Greeley tried the experiment of a penny
paper in 1833, but it failed, and it was James
Gordon Bennett, working seventeen hours a day

in a basement at 20 Wall Street, who succeeded in revolutionizing the entire newspaper "game." He had competitors in William Cullen Bryant, editor of the "Evening Post," and Benjamin Day of the "Sun," but he boldly threw over all traditions, adopted the slogan, "News, not views," reported doings on the Stock Exchange, in the churches and law courts (to the complete scandal of his readers—and he had plenty of them!) and got "scoops" on his rivals by maintaining a fast boat off Montauk Point to bring in word from European packets. Later, he employed a foreign correspondent and during the Mexican War, was one of three editors to maintain a pony express from Mobile to Montgomery, thus establishing the Associated Press.

The rioting, the general mistrust that was reflected in the newspaper controversies, the labor strikes, the unruly behavior of theatre audiences—all this unrest was suddenly given a dramatic sort of representation early in the morning of December 17, 1835. Citizens awoke to find the sky filled with smoke and flames. A fire had broken out on Merchant Street (the present Hanover) at Pearl, and was already sweeping through the warehouses and shops. The buildings in that neighborhood were mostly of wood, and flimsy in construction; and even those built of brick and stone, like the Merchants' Exchange, with its great statue of Alexander

Hamilton standing in the center of a broad corridor, were soon beyond salvaging. To increase the tragedy, water froze in the hydrants, and the firemen stood by helplessly while nearly seven hundred buildings were consumed. This, the worst of New York's long series of fires, destroyed millions of dollars worth of property and paralyzed the markets of the city. Had anyone pronounced it a blessing in disguise while its ashes were still being scattered over the surrounding streets, he would have been viewed with suspicion, but for all that, the fire of 1835 did more than anything else to secure future fire protection, improve building laws and usher in the Croton water system.

CHAPTER THIRTY-ONE

New York Speeds Up

ABOUT seventeen million dollars' worth of property had been wiped out by the fire of 1835. "These modern abominations, the gas-pipes and high buildings of four and five stories are to blame!" grumbled some; but their grumblings were ignored in the amazing real estate boom that followed. Throughout the city, new and better structures were making their appearance.

Nevertheless, something was wrong with the times. By 1837, the price of everything followed the lead of real estate. Probably President Jackson's war on the national banks had done as much harm as anything, and on February 10 of that year a huge mob of hungry citizens gathered menacingly in City Hall Park. When one of their leaders shouted that four or five hundred barrels of flour were stored in a warehouse on Washington Street, they rushed pell-mell to the place, broke in, pelted the mayor when he attempted to address them, and whitened the sidewalks with their wreckage before the police could restore order. In March, a financial panic struck New York another blow; many firms failed for large amounts. All banks stopped payments and that they were able to resume in the following year was due to the able management of James Gore King.

By 1850, New York had made improvements which erased most of the unsightly marks of fire and famine. John A. Stevens had come back from a trip to Egypt with plans of some of the tombs he had visited, and when the State appointed him as a commissioner to build a prison on the site of the old Collect Pond, he designed the original "Tombs Prison" in the Egyptian style. The second Trinity Church was torn down and the present one completed in the year 1846.

Speed became the watchword. While the Methodist Ladies' Missionary Society established their epoch-making Five Points Settlement-house to combat the evils of New York's prodigious immigration, politics began to reflect the unhappy results of a population too new and too large for its "machinery." Nevertheless, this same unwieldy array of foreigners really made possible the upbuilding of the new city. Without their labor the miles of railroad, the horse-car lines (the first in Sixth Avenue) and even the development of truck gardens in Queens, would scarcely have been possible. New York was going through a period of physical growth unparalleled in the history of cities. Fine new homes were springing up around the Washington Parade Ground; Samuel Ruggles had laid out Gramercy Park for the exclusive use of the home-owners who overlooked it, and the world of fashion was creeping up Fifth Avenue.

Many more laboring hands were needed during the years spent on the Croton water system, and by October, 1842, its completion was marked spectacularly by a great fountain near the site of the present post office in City Hall Park which shot a column of water fifty feet into the air, assuming a variety of forms. At the same time the opening of over fifty miles of aqueducts and two vast reservoirs, one in Yorkville and one on Fifth Avenue where now stands the Public Library, was celebrated in a great parade and much oratory.

Then, too, an army of workers was needed to turn the waste "goose pasture," where William Cullen Bryant loved to walk and escape from his editorial worries, into Central Park. Its wide acres had been entrusted to the artistic hands of Frederick Law Olmsted and Calvert Vaux, but years, money and above all, labor, were needed to create this noted playground.

Most important of all, the shipyards needed ten thousand men who could hammer nails, measure off miles of rope and fashion acres of sails. During seven magic years, in the very middle of the nineteenth century, the Golden Age of the clipper ship fairly bathed New York in its glow. China opened wide her ports for tea

The famous "Flying Cloud" made a new record for the trip between San Francisco and New York.

trade; Britain repealed her Navigation Laws; and California, a bit drunk with her discovery of "pay dirt," offered as high as forty-four dollars a barrel for flour.

Slender, graceful racing yachts, more skillfully built in the yards of Brooklyn and New York than anywhere else in the world, tacked and veered their way around the Horn, making new records for speed, and often clearing their construction cost in the first trip. It is true there were plenty of smoke-stacks bobbing about the wharves on the Hudson side of Manhattan. Steam navigation was being improved steadily, especially in Great Britain, but New York seemed carried away by the romantic lure of the clipper ship. Practically every international trader owned at least one, and vast wagers were laid on races to San Francisco and back. The "Sea-Witch," with her black-and-gold hull and Chinese dragon figurehead, kept the record for three years, and when the "Flying Cloud" cut it down by a few days, her exultant owner had the log of the voyage printed in gold on white silk for distribution among his friends.

The age demanded communication — ships, railroads, messages. As if the spirit of Hendrik Hudson breathed again on the banks of his river, New York had a hand in nearly all the "passageway" developments of the times. In 1853, with Cornelius Vanderbilt in control, twelve railroads took the first step toward consolidation into the Grand Central system, having its terminal in New York City. The Erie had been the first through trunk line and the Pennsylvania system was in process of organization. Back in 1839, the bulging carpet-bag of William Harnden, carrying packages back and forth between New York and Boston, had set up another kind of communication—a modest beginning for the great, diverse express business of today.

Two inventions of the period have left their indelible mark on the city's growth and industry. The sewing-machine of Elias Howe made possible quantity clothing manufacture—a kind of manufacture that takes the minimum of space in a crowded metropolis—and is therefore New York's own industry. The second invention, a "vertical screw railway," which in 1850 raised freight from floor to floor at 201 Cherry Street for Hecker Brothers, millers, was the parent of the elevator, without which four and five-story buildings could never have grown into skyscrapers of forty and fifty stories.

In such an age, it was natural that distinguished visitors should continue to appear. Barnum established a precedent for later impresarios when he charged $225 for a seat in Castle Garden at the opening concert of Jenny Lind; Charles Dickens was the recipient of the city's lavish hospitality, though later he said some rude things when he published his "American Notes." Louis Kossuth, the Hungarian patriot, was acclaimed by New York with the deepest and most sincere emotions.

In spite of such evidence of prosperity and culture as the Crystal Palace (on the site of Bryant Park) where a World's Exhibition of Industries was held in 1853, the building of the Academy of Music on Fourteenth Street and the establishment of the Philharmonic Society in 1842, panic was once more in the air. Rioting, however, was given a stern lesson in the Astor Place tragedy of 1849, when the militia, firing upon a mob gathered before the theatre to take sides in a personal feud between two actors, Forrest and Macready, killed twenty-two persons and wounded at least forty more. Rioting was checked, but unrest persisted.

By 1857, over-speculation, over-building of gallant clipper ships, and perhaps the very spirit of optimism and exaggeration that had pushed New York so far, brought a severe re-action. The Ohio Life Insurance Company failed first, precipitating about nine hundred and eighty-five other failures in the city. "Anything will make a fortune, provided it has stock to sell!" had been New York's belief too long.

CHAPTER THIRTY-TWO

Brooklyn's Famous Preacher

U P THE BOWERY one day in the early
'fifties moved a terrifying, ghostly figure
twenty feet in height, represented as trying
to break through the bonds which restrained it.
At Union Square, the figure turned left and proceeded slowly down Broadway to City Hall
Park. New York was just holding another of its
parades—but this one was grim rather than
triumphant, for the labels on the "float" read
"The Phantom of Disunion" and "Let no man
sunder the Union that God formed!"

New York's spontaneous impulse was against
the vague menace of a disrupted nation that was
already manifesting itself. On the other hand,
commercial New York has always dreaded war,
and the approaching conflict between the North
and South over slavery found its shrewd merchants no more reconciled than before to the
prospects of ruined business. It is true that New
York, nearly a quarter century earlier, had set
free its own slaves, but tolerance was an old
habit; New York wanted to encourage no abolition speeches that would menace trade with the
southern states.

In Brooklyn it was different. That gentle city,
giving her boys and girls a wide humanitarian

culture in such fine schools as the Pratt Institute, the boys' Polytechnic Institute, and the Adelphi College (the Packer Institute was not at that time a reality but only a plan) and fostering a spirit of piety in her annual Children's Day Sunday school parade, was uncompromising about abolition. For about two score years, Henry Ward Beecher was pastor of the Brooklyn Plymouth Church, swaying, as no other man of his time could, a membership of three thousand, and a visiting multitude that often overflowed into the streets. When one of these Sunday visitors asked directions to the church (for then as now one had to ask his way around Brooklyn) the answer was usually, "Cross Fulton Street and follow the crowd!"

On one fine June Sunday in 1856 the crowd was even greater than usual. Handbills and newspapers had announced an astounding event: Henry Ward Beecher intended to auction a slave girl from his own pulpit. With such dramatic effect did Beecher use the language of the slave market in bidding for the price of Sarah's freedom, that men threw their purses into the collection plate and women stripped off their jewels. Sarah's liberty was heavily over-subscribed, and the auction probably went far toward freeing others. Many years later, when Britain's attitude was bitterly hostile to the Union cause, Beecher crossed the ocean on what

*Henry Ward Beecher "sold" a slave from his pulpit
in Brooklyn.*

has been called the most remarkable embassy of all times, to win the sympathies of audience after audience that was angrily determined to prevent his very appearance.

During these years, in the very middle of the nineteenth century, Manhattan was full of many bustling interests besides abolition. The State of New York had a way of meddling in city affairs, which, to be sure, were badly managed and offered plenty of temptation to Albany legislators. One of the reforms they established was a metropolitan police force. Mayor Fernando Wood had an idea that the law was unconstitutional and determined to test it. When the new guardians of the peace appeared, he accordingly entrenched his own municipal force at the City Hall. The Seventh Regiment happened on the scene just in time to prevent more than a skirmish, and Mayor Wood, thinking that the Seventh had been dispatched by the state, and never dreaming that they were just strolling by, gracefully accepted his defeat. The metropolitan police began supervising the behavior of New York City.

The panic of 1857 had resulted in another period of desperately hard times. The poor and vicious, congested in the notorious "Gas House District" at Twenty-first Street and the East River, or in "Hell's Kitchen" in the West Thirties, formed into gangs, of which the "Dead

Rabbits" were probably the most riotous and deadly. Fortunately, there was still work for many in the Central Park grounds and this helped to tide over a period of unemployment.

An event occurred in August, 1858, that was literally, as well as figuratively, far-reaching. Years before, Cyrus W. Field had gathered together a few men of wealth and vision, among them Peter Cooper, New York's "best-loved citizen," and had explained to them the idea of a trans-Atlantic cable. In half an hour he had raised the mil-

New York hailed the first trans-Atlantic cable.

lion-and-a-half-dollar subscription that was needed. The enthusiastic dream of that little group was now a reality; everything was "set"; the Adams Express Company had pulled into place the last bit of cable; there had been cannon, speeches—and a parade. Over the wire came a message from Queen Victoria for President Buchanan, and back went his answer. Then the whole apparatus "went dead" and stayed that way for eight long, wearisome years, full of ridicule and abuse for its projectors. But New York plays the game, and eight years later the trans-Atlantic cable was a success, magically

moving Lombard Street and the Paris Bourse
next door to Wall Street, and giving the Stock
Exchange its international character. In the
meanwhile, the overland telegraph had joined
San Francisco to New York and made obsolete
the picturesque "Pony Express."

Rapid transit was again a problem in New
York, but nobody would have a car-track on
Broadway, although it took so long to reach the
new Fifth Avenue Hotel on Twenty-third Street
that many objected to its choice as a place to
entertain Edward, Prince of Wales, when he
came as a visitor in 1860.

The population lacked unity. Everyone was
looking out for himself. So fast was the city expanding, that improvements were outgrown before they were completed, and there was a con-
sequent loss of municipal pride. Civil War
seemed imminent. The New York merchants
sent petition after petition to Congress, urging
conciliation with the South. Finally, Fernando
Wood, again mayor in 1861, suggested to the
Common Council that Long Island, Staten
Island and Manhattan should secede from the
Union and form an independent state called
"Tri-Insula." The city was confused, torn by
many interests, and this situation prevailed at
the time Abraham Lincoln entered the White
House.

CHAPTER THIRTY-THREE

New York Goes to War

THE first shot fired by the secessionists on Fort Sumter cleared the air as if by magic. New York had had too much of a hand in shaping the Union to be other than patriotic at heart. Never before had there been such a mass meeting as now assembled in Union Square. It was led by John Dix, Hamilton Fish, ex-Mayor Havemeyer, and Moses Grinnell, and voted on the details of providing more money and soldiers than Lincoln had demanded. Thirty-five merchants gave equal sums to fit out the Seventh Regiment for active service.

The departure of the "Seventh" for the front was made a triumphal procession through crowded streets where the cheering never ceased for an instant. "It was worth a life, that march," wrote one of the boys. "We knew that our great city was with us as one man, utterly united in the cause we were marching to sustain!" They were the first body of New York State troops to reach Washington, and soon after went Brooklyn's famous "Fighting Fourteenth."

During the years that followed, New York saw its trim clipper-ships driven from the seas, and its steam lines pass into the registry of Great Britain. The members of the Stock Exchange, foreseeing a possibility of speculating in gold, pledged themselves against it; but profits were high in other forms of commerce. New York gained rather than lost in wealth.

The city gave generously of both wealth and men to the Union cause; nor did organization and invention lag. The Union League Club was founded in 1862 to aid recruiting, and the "Monitor," a new model ironclad, invented by John Ericsson, was launched at Greenpoint, Long Island.

In 1863, the same year that the National Bank Act made New York a money reservoir for the government, all available troops were sent from the city to the front, leaving a lawless element in control. This unfortunate state of affairs, coupled with the passage of the Draft Act on July 13, produced the most terrible uprising in the city's history. Since it permitted men to purchase exemption from military service, the Draft Act was prejudicial to the poor—and the fury of the vicious element was at once directed against the innocent negroes in the city. For four days the rioting went on; over a million dollars' worth of property was destroyed, and twelve hundred lives were lost.

With the aid of volunteers from Brooklyn, the local police gained control by the time the soldiers were rushed back to the city's defense. Later a public fund was provided to purchase exemption for those who were unable to care for their dependents.

On the twelfth day of April, 1865, following the surrender of Lee at Appomattox, seventy-five Brooklyn citizens made a joyous pilgrimage to Fort Sumter to hoist the Union Flag and listen to an address by Beecher; but their holiday spirits on the return trip turned to horror at the sudden news of Lincoln's assassination.

At the same moment this same dire news had brought together an almost hysterical mob in Wall Street, and from the steps of the Sub-Treasury Building, Garfield made his brief, inspired address that averted a threatened panic.

The city's last respects to the martyred President were paid on April 24, when the body, on its way to a final resting place in Springfield, Illinois, lay in state in the governor's room of the City Hall. On the following day it was carried through the streets to the Hudson River Railroad Depot, escorted by a mourning cortege five miles long. It was with no feeling of triumph that New York City returned to the routine of peace.

CHAPTER THIRTY-FOUR

Growing Pains

THREE times had New York gone into war, and always reluctantly. Now, for the third time the city emerged from conflict and, just as in the two earlier cases, with unexpected gains. Each struggle had registered its own peculiar change in the city's life. The close of the Revolutionary War gave New York the commercial, financial, and for a time the political leadership of the new nation; while after the War of 1812 there followed "clipper ship" supremacy that poured wealth into its coffers.

The Civil War left an even greater impress. Wall Street had been an important "battlefield" of the Civil War; here had originated the plans for advertising the sale of government bonds to meet the expenses of the conflict, and from Wall Street President Lincoln had called John A. Stewart to be Assistant Secretary of the Treasury. American leadership in the ocean-carrying trade was gone, but in its place came a tremendous urge toward internal development; the country entered an age of machines, of factories and particularly of railroad expansion.

At the close of the war, therefore, when nation-wide development called for financing on a huge scale, Wall Street became the natural

*The memorable "Black Friday" panic took place
on the New York Stock Exchange.*

center for such activity. Business became extremely active, and there arose financial giants who entered eagerly into the task of piecing together small, privately owned railroads into colossal systems—such men as Vanderbilt, Huntington, Gould and Fiske, and, in more recent years, Hill and Harriman. Safe and sound stock investments mingled on the market with much furious and precarious gambling. Fortunes were made and lost, but through it all, the growth of the railroads proceeded rapidly, opening up new regions to travel and commerce and bringing prosperity to many sections of the country.

Side by side with this stimulus to commerce, a certain amount of demoralization followed the Civil War, and this showed most intensively in New York City, because here business intensity is greatest. People felt that the day of small things had come to an end, and that the day of opportunity had arrived. To some, this meant constructive enterprise of lasting benefit to the country, but to many others it meant a chance to make some big "killings."

In the fall of 1869, one such predatory group conceived the idea of cornering the gold market, and quietly began buying in all the specie. Everything was proceeding merrily; the price of gold was being forced up and up to giddy, dangerous heights, and then, suddenly, between 11:50 A.M. and 12:11 P.M. on September 24, prices crashed amid wildest confusion. This disastrous day, on which thousands of speculators were ruined, became known as "Black Friday," and it was not learned until years later that Henry Clews, alarmed at the reckless actions of the pool, had sent a telegram to President Grant asking him to act. The President's response had been the release of five million dollars in gold, an amount sufficient to smash the pool.

In many other instances of lawless raiding, particularly in railroad stocks, the unscrupulous speculator had his own way quite unchecked—between the bulls and the bears thus turned wolves, the lambs suffered.

However, it was in politics even more than in finance that the city's "growing pains" were felt. New York City government fell into the hands of a new type of buccaneer. Under "Boss" Tweed and his "Ring" of pirates, distinguishable by waxed moustaches and large diamond stick pins rather than sashes and daggers, the cost of public improvements rose to astonishing figures. In the construction of the new County Court House which still stands on the northern part of City Hall Park, the most brazen profits were taken by the Ring: $641,000 was charged for its carpets, $1,937,545 for plastering and frescoing, and $2,960,187 for furniture and cabinet work, and similar amounts for other items.

Finally, when corrupt rule had cost the tax-
payers about $160,000,000, the city grew weary
of walking the plank. George Jones, the editor
of the "New York Times," Thomas Nast, the
famous cartoonist of "Harper's Weekly," and
Samuel J. Tilden, founder of the New York
Bar Association, led a vigorous attack on the
political bandits and overthrew them. "Boss"
Tweed died in jail.

That New York grew steadily through all
the years of feverish speculation and political
corruption, is fur-
ther proof of its high
commercial destiny.
The city had passed
the million mark in
population, and
there was a great de-
mand for rapid tran-
sit on the long and
narrow island of

In the early days of the "L".

Manhattan. To meet this situation, the elevated
railroad arose, section by section, above the
crowded streets. There was even one little experimental subway tunnel dug under Broadway
from Murray Street to Park Place—but it was
abandoned as impracticable.

In 1870, New York's huge energy found another expression. Work was commenced on the
mighty Brooklyn Bridge, and three years later,

when the city pushed its boundary northward as far as Yonkers, the need was felt for other bridges to span the Harlem River as well as the East River.

Meanwhile the big town was not neglecting culture. The Metropolitan Museum of Art was founded in 1870; and, with the creation of a Board of Education and the voting of school bonds, it became possible to establish normal schools and evening high schools. The Lenox Library was founded, in addition to the Astor Library, which had existed since 1848; and Joseph Jefferson's "Rip Van Winkle" was attracting crowds to Booth's Theatre on Twenty-third Street.

Nor was the exposure of the Tweed Ring the only great newspaper exploit of the day. James Gordon Bennett of the "New York Herald" financed an African expedition under Henry M. Stanley to search for David Livingstone, the missionary. After thrilling adventures, this expedition accomplished its task in November, 1871, thus giving to the world all of Livingstone's maps and journals about that unknown territory.

In 1873, New York suffered again from its "growing pains," this time provoked by its cultivated sensitiveness to foreign market conditions. South American and Russian wheat began competing with home crops, and with the opening of the Suez Canal, trade routes were upset. Added to these conditions abroad, there was again overspeculation in railroads at home. A panic greater than those which had closed the banks and paralyzed trade in previous years fell upon the city, and this time it took the merchants ten years to recover from its depressing effects.

CHAPTER THIRTY-FIVE

A Strange Fulfillment

A PASSAGEWAY to the Pacific had been Hendrik Hudson's dream away back in 1609 when he sighted the island of "Manna-hatin"—just as it had inspired Columbus with daring over a hundred years earlier. Both men had failed; yet the dreams of courageous men never seem to die. In 1876, the ambition of Hendrik Hudson was strangely fulfilled.

"De Halve Maen" had brought commerce to the island at the mouth of the Hudson River, and it had taken deep root. Born in commerce, the City of New York thought in terms of commerce and grew through commerce. Just as Hudson had been carried across the sea by his adventurous energy, the city that sprang from his voyage inherited the power to think in vast terms, to over-ride all cost and difficulty in carrying out its ambitious plans. Before 1850 it had conquered the ocean for its commerce; in the 60's it turned inland in its search for markets and now in 1876 its railroad magnates achieved their great ambition by sending a through train from New York to San Francisco in eighty-three hours and forty-three minutes. Thus the passage from sea to sea was at last accomplished. The way to the Orient, of which Hudson had dreamed, was found by men who came after him and dwelt and dreamed on the island of his discovery. The goal was the same; the route was different.

This was a great year for all Americans, because it marked the one hundredth anniversary of American independence. No longer was the United States to be reckoned as a "new" nation; its government already was older than that of the Republic of France, the Empire of Germany or the Kingdom of Italy. Yet its chief city was still young in comparison with the great cities of Europe which it was rapidly outgrowing. New York was an astounding, youthful giant, but with all its optimism, it had not begun to realize the grandeur of its destiny.

In those days, most of its business section was still at the "four-story level," because elevators were few and unsatisfactory and people would not climb too many flights of stairs. There were no telephones; in fact, it was not until August 5, 1877, that the "New York Sun" published exultantly, as a bit of up-to-the-minute news, that there were five working telephones in the city. Prospective customers were soon to be encouraged with the offer of a month's free trial.

Edison had not yet produced his electric lamp, and the term "gas light" still sounded very modern. In many hotels were to be found cards warning the guests not to blow out the gas.

However, obstacles to progress were disappearing right and left. On September 24, 1876, General Nelson's little daughter had pressed a button, and mines that took ten years in the laying, blew up a deadly reef in Hell Gate Channel. One by one, the channel's teeth were extracted in this fashion, until, in 1885, the last nine acres of jagged rock crumbled to harmless bits. Ten years later the Harlem Ship Canal was completed, and with the planning of new piers, bridges and terminals, and the opening of American trans-Atlantic steamship lines, New York was well on its way toward the modern idea of a Port Authority District.

Litigation about the surface car lines had been another obstacle to progress, and with its settlement trolley-cars were presently rattling up Amsterdam Avenue or crossing the Brooklyn Bridge. Many living New Yorkers will remember that at the time this seemed an extraordinary achievement—a marvel of speedy and convenient transportation.

CHAPTER THIRTY-SIX

Bicycle Days

SAILBOATS and steamboats, locomotives, horse cars and trolley-cars—all these had played their part in the development of New York. Now, during the "eighties" and "nineties," a new kind of vehicle carried the city onward still another step. As early as 1877, the high wheel had made its appearance on the streets and even before that the old "boneshaker" was not unknown, but it was not until the coming of the low-wheeled "safety" that the craze really took hold. Then the influence of tens of thousands of cyclists began to make itself felt with power. Cobblestones gave way to asphalt, along which the endless procession could speed with pleasure, and recreation parks were created far enough away to meet the demand for outings. Bronx, Pelham Bay, Van Cortlandt and other parks owed much of their planning to the bicycle vogue; and along beautiful new Riverside Drive, on almost any summer evening, a myriad of twinkling headlights moved in a glowing, shifting, dreamy maze. In those days, the Duke of Marlborough, perhaps on courtship bound, was arrested for "scorching on his bike," and young Alfred E. Smith won his first popular title of "Coaster King."

*New York unveiled "Liberty Enlightening the World," a
gift to this nation from the people of France.*

But the city had problems as well as pleasures. A Russian Czar, Alexander III, began to persecute the Jews in his empire, and thousands of them fled to New York, where they added to the difficulties of the congested districts, particularly of the East Side. The problem from over-immigration was already acute, for races had formed the habit of huddling in separate communities, and crowded tenement houses of the "dumb-bell" airshaft design offered a direct challenge to the city's health. In 1879, a mass meeting of citizens in Cooper Union resulted in the formation of the "Improved Dwelling Association" and the making of sanitary laws; while in Brooklyn, Alfred T. White set a new standard with his home buildings constructed around a central court. Castle Garden had served for a time as an immigrant station, and it was not until 1892 that Ellis Island was purchased and fitted up for the reception of the oncoming wave of foreigners.

Perhaps it was the big Brooklyn Bridge that gave the city a greater urge toward permanence and beauty in its buildings. At any rate, the old brownstone fronts began to give way to the "chateau" type of mansion after the middle of the century and there was greater enthusiasm for public monuments and edifices. St. Patrick's Cathedral, on Fifth Avenue between Fiftieth and Fifty-first Streets, was dedicated in 1879 by

Cardinal McCloskey, whose father had given so generously to the founding of St. James Cathedral, Brooklyn's first Catholic Church. There soon followed the Temple Beth-El, and the Episcopal Church of St. Thomas. The Architectural League of New York dates from 1881, with Meade, McKim, Tiffany, Le Brun, St. Gaudens, Lefarge and such other first-rate names among its membership.

In the very year that marked the completion of Brooklyn Bridge, 1883, the first Metropolitan Opera House was opened with a brilliant performance of "Faust;" and a gala benefit was held in the Fourteenth Street Academy of Music to provide a pedestal for the statue of "Liberty Enlightening the World," a gift of the people of France to this nation. Then, on November 26, the centennial of British evacuation was celebrated by placing a statue of Washington, donated by the merchants of New York, on the steps of the Sub-Treasury Building, the site of his inauguration as first President under the Constitution of the United States.

Another memorial, planned in 1885, was designed to commemorate still another President whose death stirred the city's deepest emotions. Ulysses S. Grant, under shadow of death, spent his last days painfully writing his memoirs to provide an estate for his wife. For his remains a small tomb was erected on the banks of the

Hudson River. To this site, a mourning cortege, six miles in length, bore the body on August 7, after it had lain in state for three days in the draped rotunda of the City Hall. In 1897, the present stately monument, although not completed, was dedicated to his memory.

"Liberty" mounted her pedestal on October 28, 1896. Senator Evart's speech was left unfinished because a premature signal lowered the veiling flag when he had scarcely begun. Through the campaign efforts of the "New York World," which had been so active in securing

The "Great Blizzard of '88" struck New York and raged furiously for three days, tying up business and traffic.

funds for the pedestal, the statue was equipped to shed a radiant electric light through the torch and tiara.

Theatres gradually edged their way uptown from the old "Rialto" on Fourteenth Street, and with this northwesterly movement, the great stock companies of Lester Wallack, Augustin Daly, and the Frohmans began to change into the modern "star" system. The spotlight already had lingered upon Booth and Barrett, Ada Rehan, Modjeska and Mansfield, John Drew and Mary Anderson, while across the Atlantic came Bernhardt, Duse, Henry Irving, Ellen Terry and other famous players, to make New York first in theatrical importance among American cities and establish its prestige as a mecca for foreign talent.

On March 11, 1888, when the "cloak and suit" manufacturers had every right to anticipate a noble spring parade of Fifth Avenue fashionables, the Great Blizzard struck New York instead, raging furiously for three days, tying up business and traffic with its twenty-two inches of snow and causing acute distress.

The Washington Centennial of 1889 was a three-day jubilee which re-enacted the old scenes of Wall Street's Federal glory. President Harrison was rowed from Elizabethtown, as Washington had been, in a decorated barge. The ceremonies of the day were made impressive by an ode of Whittier's and a speech by Chauncey Depew, who was then a prominent figure in the financial and political life of the city.

Later, the beautiful arch in Washington Square, designed by Stanford White and inspired by the Centennial celebration, gave a more lasting expression to New York's reverence for this hero of the past.

CHAPTER THIRTY-SEVEN

The Birth of Greater New York

ANDREW H. GREEN of Brooklyn was a most remarkable man. During the nineteenth century, his inexhaustible public spirit was poured into the founding of the Metropolitan Museum of Art, the New York Public Library, the American Museum of Natural History, the New York Zoological Society and the establishment of Central Park. It was, however, in 1868, soon after the Civil War, that he had conceived his most magnificent idea, that of creating a Greater City of New York, and from this idea, as well as the thirty years of labor he devoted to making it a reality, he gained the title by which he is best known, "The Father of Greater New York."

The same year that saw New York's population leap to the million-and-a-half mark, having doubled itself in the preceding quarter century, found the legislators ready to entertain Andrew Green's idea. In 1890 a commission was appointed to work upon the subject. It was during this period of the commission's deliberations that New York began to create its soaring "skyline." Four or five stories had satisfied most builders up to now; ten stories constituted a tall building, and more than ten was a "sky-scraper."

A visitor coming to New York on one of the
North River ferries in 1890 would have seen
the square red tower of the Produce Exchange,
the spires of Trinity and St. Paul's Churches, the
sharp pointed Tribune Tower, the brilliant gold
dome of the new Pulitzer (World) Building,
and the towers of the Brooklyn Bridge rearing
themselves above the general level of other
buildings in the city.

Now several influences caused New York to
reach for the clouds. One was the pressure of
population on a long, narrow island where in
the downtown section, every available square
foot of ground was already covered by the old-
type buildings. Business filled these from basement to roof, and still the demand for more
space grew. Commerce had made New York;
now it seemed to be strangling it. Concerns from
all parts of the country felt it necessary to open
offices in the city which dominated shipping
and finance. Space they must have, whatever
the cost. There was only one answer: Put offices
on top of offices. Go higher!

Fortunately, elevators were improving and
people were more willing than formerly to ride
in them to upper floors; fortunately, also, steel
construction was solving the problem of gaining
sufficient strength without using precious ground
space for massive walls. These three factors,
commerce, elevators and steel construction, now

*Andrew H. Green advocated the formation of
Greater New York*

caused a strange new city to grow upon the ground that had been trod by bartering Indians and Revolutionary patriots. Higher and higher rose the buildings until, as the century closed, the twenty-six stories of the Park Row Building seemed a limit of human achievement.

In the mean time, residences were following one another farther north, and northward followed also the retail stores. Fashion, when well established in Fifth and Madison Avenues, began to extend beyond Fifty-ninth Street. Twenty-third Street succeeded Fourteenth, as it in turn had displaced Grand Street as the leading shopping district. The "Big Store" at Sixth Avenue and Eighteenth Street seemed almost unbelievably vast, and Tiffany's began to think of migrating from Union Square. A cartoon of the period showed the average New Yorker with all his goods packed on a camel, starting out on a road marked "Farther north."

Now came a generation of new hotels, forerunners of future hundreds. The Waldorf (later to build itself an "Astoria" alongside), the first Plaza, the Netherlands and the Savoy, became the "grand" hostelries. Society was supposed to consist of the "Four Hundred," ruled by Mrs. Astor and Ward McAllister, but the multitude outside of this exclusive group were busily engaged in creating the real city and doing its worthwhile work.

This was the time of the cable-cars which swooped around "Dead Man's Curve" at Broadway and Fourteenth Street, of the "Gibson Girl," the "Floradora Sextette," and also of the growing pressure of city transportation. "The rapid transit problem," wrote Mayor Gilroy in his message of 1894, "is no nearer solution than it was two years ago." Two years earlier had been born the story of the Uptown Commuter— that famous Mr. Brown who came home from business one day and met his offspring at the dinner table. "This is your father," Mrs. Brown is reputed to have said. "I am very glad to meet you, sir," responded the son with formal dignity. "I have often heard my mother speak of you." To supply the need of faster travel in town, a Rapid Transit Commission was appointed in 1894, with Seth Low and Alexander Orr among its members, and the Commission's engineer, William Barclay Parsons, was dispatched to Europe to spend a year in study of foreign transit conditions.

The "nineties" had also their great social and political upheaval, not unlike that which had toppled Tweed. Dr. Parkhurst, a Presbyterian clergyman, made during this time an investigation of New York's underworld, and early in 1892 exposed an alliance between politics and organized vice. When all the evidence was brought to light before the Lexow Committee of the legislature, the public indignation awoke. A reform ticket, headed by William L. Strong, was swept into power on November 6, 1894.

Mayor Strong was the last to preside over old New York. The Greater New York Commission finally made its report, recommending that Brooklyn and the territories now contained in Queens and Richmond be combined with Manhattan and the Bronx into one great municipality. In spite of the vetoes of two mayors, the legislature passed the recommendation and appointed a committee to draw up a charter. Thus, five years before his long and useful life was ended by the bullet of a crazed assassin, the venerable Andrew Green saw his dream come true: in 1898 a new city of more than three million inhabitants took its place among the world's great commercial centers. New York welcomed the twentieth century with a wider vision than ever.

CHAPTER THIRTY-EIGHT

The Subway Comes

FIGURATIVELY speaking, people took a deep breath at the dawn of the twentieth century; they forgot the past and began to look ahead. New York, the City of the Future, has always strongly felt the spirit of progress. Again it rejuvenated itself; "Greater" New York plunged into fresh activity.

Its first great problem was that of transportation. The five boroughs covered nearly two hundred thousand acres, and included former cities, towns and villages that were just learning to think and act together as one municipality. Their people must be able to move back and forth without such great delay. Besides, with business continuing to concentrate in the lower part of Manhattan, it became necessary for the majority of people to travel even greater distances between their homes and offices. The surface-cars and elevated had long been over-crowded. Now, after much deliberation, New York embarked upon the tremendous project of subway construction, and the first spadeful of earth was turned by the mayor in front of the City Hall on March 24, in the year 1900.

Of course there followed a distressing period of dirt and disorder. A great open ditch bordered by rough board fences was dug through some of the busiest streets. Thunderous blasts tore into the city's rock foundation, and did no small amount of damage above ground. Wagons hauled away dirt and stone to help build up Long Island City and other parts of the "Greater" unit, while along the subway route it looked as if an earthquake had visited the rocky island of Manhattan. Nearly every one suffered inconvenience and even financial loss, but on the whole, took it philosophically because it was the price of progress. Then, after a while,

the contractors learned to board over the cut during traffic hours, and the additional subways began to cause less discomfort.

New York built subways.

In the fall of 1904, the subway was ready for travel. Delighted New Yorkers poured into the openings in such great numbers that facilities designed to handle four hundred thousand people a day were ultimately jammed with more than twice that number. It became and, in spite of the great extension of the system, still continues to be, an ordeal to travel during the "rush hours;" but it did furnish really rapid transit. It be-

gan to knit together distant parts of the city—
a weaving process that still continues, while the
city's increase in population keeps always a long
step ahead of it.

In the beginning, few realized what a mighty
city-building influence the subway was to exert.
It had been planned to bring the first line down
Broadway below Forty-second Street, but property owners raised objections and succeeded in
having it diverted to Park Avenue, Fourth Avenue and Lafayette Street. These property owners were spared the annoyance of the open cut,
particularly in the great textile and clothing districts north of Duane Street, and for a short time
they enjoyed their triumph. Then some real
estate operators were struck with a bold idea.
Why not make it easier for buyers to reach their
trades by locating them along the subway? Accordingly, big modern loft and office buildings
with high ceilings, large windows, good elevator
service and fire sprinkler protection began to
rise along Fourth Avenue. The tenants of the
dingy, antiquated buildings in the old district
required little persuasion to move. They left in
such numbers that block after block became almost depopulated and the value of property
dropped alarmingly. Later, when other subway
lines were projected, property owners in the
vicinity welcomed them with open arms.

Additional bridges were flung across to Long

Island. Even the Brooklyn Bridge, a few years earlier the wonder of the world, was exceeded in total length by the Williamsburg Bridge, which was opened in 1903; and during the next nine years, the Manhattan, the Queensborough and the Hell Gate bridges took still longer leaps across the East River. An age of science, of mechanical devices, of research and enlightenment was upon the world, and in a very high degree this was evidenced by activities of New York.

When the Greater City was started, it was hampered politically because of the scattering of responsibilities and powers, so that the need of a new charter soon became evident. By 1901 a charter was granted which provided for greater centralization by centering authority in the mayor and a board of apportionment. Moreover, certain important new departments were established, one of which was the Art Commission—the first of its kind in any city—whose purpose it was to keep an expert eye upon a growth in beauty in such undertakings as monuments and public buildings. In 1907, a Bureau of Municipal Research was created in response to the general demand, for specific and accurate knowledge both in business and government was being generally manifested. Columbia College, since 1891 in its present location, had graduated into a university, and Seth Low, its president and the second mayor of the Greater City, later bequeathed to it the Low Memorial Library. Charles B. Snyder was elected Superintendent of School Buildings in 1891, and continued in office for over thirty years, giving to the city a system of buildings that has furnished the model for educational institutions throughout the United States.

The passion for better living conditions and enlightenment prompted many large benefactions in the form of "foundations." In 1903, Joseph Pulitzer of the "New York World" founded the Columbia University School of Journalism. The Russell Sage and Rockefeller foundations, the Altman and other bequests to the Metropolitan Museum and the Museum of Natural History, and the various Carnegie gifts, have not only raised the standards of human thought and life, but they have also encouraged countless other donors in many fields.

CHAPTER THIRTY-NINE

A Birthday Celebration

ALTHOUGH there had been much flag-flying and marching at home, the guns of the Spanish War in 1898 were too far away and too quickly silenced to affect New York very deeply. Yet out of that brief, distant conflict America emerged a world power with new interests in the affairs of other continents. New York, with its cosmopolitan population and its great foreign trade, felt this influence more keenly than most other sections of the country. The Spanish War had also made a New Yorker President of the United States. Theodore Roosevelt, who was born on East Twentieth Street, and who, with Leonard Wood, led the dashing "Rough Riders" in the Cuban campaign, was elected governor of the state on his war record, then was drafted against his will for the vice-presidential nomination in 1900, and finally, on the assassination of President McKinley, became his successor.

However, in the peace of the early twentieth century, New York was busied with its own affairs. The term for mayor, comptroller and borough presidents was extended to four years; the city had learned a lesson about expanding the government to fit its growth in other direc-

tions. The "Times" moved into its new home
on the square named for it, just as Broadway
electric signs began to present a dazzling spec-
tacle in the "Great White Way." In one year,
New York consumed four times the electric current needed for Greater London!

Improvements in the city's water system had
been keeping abreast of the public need by
means of new underground aqueducts and tap-
ping of the Bronx River, but by 1907 something
more was needed and construction began on a
great project to bring an enormous new supply
from the Catskill Mountains.

A new municipal building was needed, and
competition for its plans had a distinct effect on
the modern New York skyscraper. While the
vast edifice arose to overlook City Hall Park
from the northeast, Mrs. Russell Sage's gener-
osity made possible an authentic restoration of
the beautiful old City Hall, so closely associated
with the eventful De Witt Clinton period of
state and city history.

There was now a desire felt to preserve and
refurbish the city's historic landmarks. Old
Fraunces' Tavern was made over into its like-
ness of the days when Washington spoke his
farewell to his generals.

In the midst of all this bustle of tearing down,
building, digging and reconstruction, the Knickerbocker Trust Company failed in 1907, caus-

ing a panic in Wall Street; but this time the Clearing House, J. Pierpont Morgan, the financial magnate, and the U. S. Treasury came quickly to the rescue.

In 1909, New York celebrated a great anniversary. Three hundred years had passed since Hudson guided his Dutch "yacht" up an unknown river, and one hundred since Robert Fulton followed his path in a steamboat. New York therefore gave a party and all the world was invited. From Amsterdam came a little replica of "The Half Moon;" the battle cruisers from the other great nations joined our Atlantic Fleet in a great naval procession up the Hudson River on September 25. The "Half Moon," manned by Dutch sailors in the dress of Hudson's time, and a reproduction of the "Clermont," crowded by celebrities representing Fulton and his friends, were escorted through the Kill van Kull into the lower harbor and led this most brilliant naval pageant the world has ever known.

For two weeks the city's life was an exciting series of parades and unveilings by day, and fireworks, balls and banquets by night. Verrazzano was not forgotten in the celebration of the city's discovery, and a statue of that explorer was dedicated at the Battery; one of Hudson was unveiled on Spuyten Duyvil Hill, and a bust of Fulton was placed in the new hall of Fame at New York University. The Japanese citizens

During the Hudson-Fulton celebration Wilbur Wright made a spectacular flight over the Hudson in his new airship.

presented Riverside Drive with a grove of cherry trees and, most momentous of all, Wilbur Wright flew up the Hudson in his airship from Governor's Island to Grant's Tomb and back, thus sounding a prophetic note of the future through all this reawakened fervor for the glorious past. Visitors who attended the celebration found other attractions as well—the new tubes to Brooklyn and Jersey, or the wonderful skyscrapers like the Singer Building and the Metropolitan Tower that had already been erected.

As the last visiting cruiser departed, New York returned with greater zeal than ever to its program of tearing down and rebuilding. St. Patrick's beautiful spires were complete in 1910; the church of St. John the Divine was slowly taking form on Morningside Heights; and by 1913 the present Grand Central Terminal was opened.

With the dawn of 1914, Mayor John Purroy Mitchel came into office. He proved to be a new sort of executive who demanded experts and modern methods of research and accounting in every department of his business-like administration. Modern science and technology had already been very strongly evident in the administration of Mayor McClellan. Major W. C. Gorgas, who had received part of his medical education at Bellevue, completed his successful warfare against fever at Panama, and the Canal was opened to form a new waterway from New York to the Orient.

Across the Atlantic, however, destruction was in the air, and this same year, 1914, saw the war-cloud break, precipitating its deluge. With news of war, the Cotton, Produce and Stock Exchanges closed their doors, and again panic threatened in New York. It was only a threat, for the Federal Reserve Law was hurried through, the emergency was met and the market stabilized. Out of the deluge, New York was destined to emerge as the "cash drawer of the world."

CHAPTER FORTY

War and Peace

IN SPITE of the fact that actual fighting took place more than three thousand miles away, it will take many years to form a just estimate of the tremendous effect of the world convulsion upon this city.

For significant things have happened to New York since 1914!

During the two nervous years of neutrality following Germany's invasion of Belgium, New York, as the vast port through which went food, supplies and ammunition to the belligerents, watched civic disturbances increase along with its wealth. There were bomb plots and rumors of bomb plots, strikes for higher wages, strikes for shorter hours, strikes for better working conditions. On the 7th of May, 1915, when the "Lusitania" was torpedoed by a German submarine and sank, she carried to the bottom many New Yorkers, among them Alfred G. Vanderbilt and Charles Frohman; and so through all the talk of peace, there sounded the sinister rumbles of war.

Citizens held a Preparedness Parade and President Wilson, accompanied by Secretary Daniels, came to review the United States Fleet at anchor in the Hudson River. A thirty-foot channel,

authorized by the Federal Government, was dug
through Hell Gate from Long Island Sound to
the Brooklyn Navy Yard, for the passage of
battle cruisers, and even the German merchant
submarine, the "Deutschland," came a-market-
ing to this port.

During this period when war was thundering
on hundreds of miles of European battlefronts,
the United States at large was undoubtedly pros-
pering and New York to a higher degree than
ever before in its history. At the close of 1916,
the Stock Exchange was transacting the greatest volume of business in fifteen years. American exports passing through the port were fairly doubling those of other years, and the city's
requisition of stamps from the Post Office Department for the year 1917 alone, if placed in
a single stack, would have reached to four times
the height of the Washington Monument.

The Ashokan Reservoir of the mammoth
Catskill Water Project was opened in 1917, and
by 1924, when the Gilboa Dam and the Shan-
daken Tunnel (the world's longest) were complete, the city had executed an engineering feat
rivaling the Panama Canal itself.

But in the meanwhile, the approach of conflict was more and more unmistakable. On April
6, 1917, the United States declared war upon
Germany, and New York revived its ancient
role as ship-builder, under the direction of

Charles M. Schwab, and entered upon the heart-
rending task of seeing off to the front the "fighting men of '17."

Then followed wheatless and heatless days,
lightless nights and finally motorless Sundays.
The city's troubles were increased by long-
shoremen's strikes, fires of incendiary origin,
and the scourge of the Spanish influenza. For
the duration of the war, work was suspended on
all churches, hotels, schools, theatres and other
public buildings, and New York bent its energies toward sending well over the top each of the
five successful Liberty Loan drives, furnishing
about one-fourth of the total sum of the country's war expenditure. Such citizens as John D.
Ryan, Albert Rathbone, Albert Strauss, Rodman
Wanamaker and Elihu Root were called into
executive positions; while, on the other hand,
among the war's casualties, ex-Mayor Mitchel
lost his life on the aviation field at Lake Charles,
an event mourned by the entire city.

On November 7, 1918, an erroneous press
cable message, received at New York about one
o'clock P.M. set all the sirens and bells to shrieking in a wild delirium of joy. Extras rushed out
with the headlines "Germany surrenders! The
War is over!" but already the wild celebration
of New York's false Armistice Day was in
full swing. Schools were dismissed and all business stopped. Everything that could make a

noise, from a paper-covered comb to a steam whistle added its voice to the city's uproar. Apparently with one accord, dozens of downtown office buildings began to dump the contents of waste baskets from thousands of windows. At times, the air was darkened by the dense paper snowfall, which piled up deep underfoot, and literally miles of ticker-tape were sent spinning from innumerable brokers' windows to cling in gigantic paper cobwebs to the tall buildings.

Fifth Avenue for at least three miles was jammed solidly from curb to curb with dancing, shrieking humanity. Sedate old gentlemen smashed their derbies and turned their overcoats inside out, and refined ladies went about kissing every uniformed man they met. On a balcony of the Knickerbocker Hotel appeared Caruso, waving a flag and singing "The Star Spangled Banner" to probably his only audience that ever was too thrilled by its own emotions to listen.

By evening, when the news was denied, reality, strangely enough could not destroy New York's high spirits and hope. From then on until November 11, the time was spent in eager anticipation of peace. Word of the signing of the armistice came through at 3 o'clock that morning, and searchlights and sirens announced it to the city. Once more people gathered, but this time a little more deliberately, to celebrate the return of peace.

Up Fifth Avenue marched New York's "Own" the Twenty-seventh Division, returning from the Great War.

In 1919, wave after wave of the returning divisions of American soldiers, sailors, marines, passed through New York, and not one failed to received its royal welcome. On February 17, to the blare of Jim Europe's jazz band, the 369th Infantry (the old Fifteenth Colored) marched up Fifth Avenue to Harlem, its home, the only New York organization that had served throughout under its own State colors. It carried 191 citations for individual gallantry; the Croix de Guerre had been bestowed upon its colors for signal bravery during the Meuse-Argonne offensive; while through the courtesy of the French it had been the first regiment of the Allies to reach the Rhine.

For the welcome of New York's "Own," the Twenty-seventh Division (an outgrowth of the old National Guard), a grand stand was erected from Sixtieth Street to One Hundred and Tenth Street, and on March 25, five miles of soldiers, under such perfect discipline that they seemed all unconscious of the tumult about them, ignoring the shower of blossoms, fruit and banknotes, marched behind Major-General John F. O'Ryan, in what has been called the "grimness that won, rather than the jubilation of victory." A huge Arch of Victory, with a Court of the Heroic Dead, spanned their way at Madison Square, and another, an Arch of Jewels, at Fifty-ninth Street. The largest crowd that had ever gathered in New York sought places along the line of march from daybreak on. Gold stars —1,972 of them—indicated what gaps there were in the columns that filed past the reviewing-stand where Governor Alfred E. Smith and other public officials stood. Overhead, circled airplanes—"at one time as many as five!"

The Seventy-seventh Division with its Chinese standard-bearer, typifying the racial diversity that made it also New York's own—the product of a city which reads its newspapers in twenty languages, which has more Irish than Dublin, more Italians than any city but Rome, and which contains the largest Jewish population in the world—came back on May 6. Then the final great outburst of welcoming fervor was lavished on General Pershing as he led the famous First Division, twenty-five thousand strong, through an avenue strewn deep with laurel and flower petals. Above the pealing of church bells and the triumphant music of bands, rose shouts for the great popular war leader. With drums muffled and colors dipped for the dead, the division swept through the Victory Arch, and on the steps of St. Patrick's Cathedral, Cardinal Mercier of Belgium stood beside Cardinal Hayes (then Archbishop) to watch the city's last great parade for its returning soldiers, a parade which Pershing declared was "the most enthusiastic patriotic outburst that could be imagined."

CHAPTER FORTY-ONE

Becoming Air-Minded

THE fact that New York City had much of the world's gold in its cash drawer by 1920 added somewhat to the perils of its reconstruction period. High wartime wages had encouraged men to live extravagantly, and personal speculation began to take much of the capital that had been devoted before in a more direct way to the expansion of business. The same unrest that made royalties and other distinguished persons come in greater numbers than ever to visit New York now that peace had returned, stirred through every class of society. While New York offered its freedom, in turn, to the royal family of Belgium, to Marshal Foch and Prince Aage of Denmark, and even permitted the Prince of Wales to hang on a subway strap, something very near anarchy showed its ugly head about the city.

There had been war profiteering, and there continued to be construction "graft." The cost of living soared higher and higher, to bring more discontent. In spite of work on public improvements, like the Queensborough subway tunnel, the Bronx River Parkway, the Broadway-Brighton subway extension, and many other rapid transit developments, there was unemployment, and many rumors of "Red" plots filled the air. Then, on September 16, 1920, the most serious bomb explosion in the city's history occurred in front of the U. S. Assay Office near the corner of Broad and Wall Streets, in which thirty-three persons were killed and more than three hundred were wounded. The explosives had been conveyed to the spot in a one-horse truck and set off at noon, blowing the horse and vehicle to atoms, shattering windows, hurling bits of masonry through the air, and strewing the pavement with dead and dying.

The horror of this outrage, which many were ready to blame on the discontent that was drifting over from unhappy northern Europe, made the national law restricting immigration doubly welcome to New York, and the importance of this regulation can hardly be over-estimated, providing, as it does, a chance for the city to catch up a bit with its "ingredients."

In 1921, the same year in which this law was passed, a treaty between New York and New Jersey—the result of a Port and Harbor Commission appointed in 1917, created a Port Authority Board, whose plans for development were promptly approved by the state and federal officials. The port projects are courageous and farseeing, worthy of the great gateway through which pass 50 per cent. of the country's imports and 40 per cent. of its exports. They call for the establishment of nine vast terminal freight stations in Manhattan, the development of Jamaica Bay for ocean ships and for many other great improvements.

Clemenceau was the city's guest in 1922, and in Brooklyn was greeted by three hundred thousand school children, while Paderewski came back to the concert stage in Carnegie Hall, rejoining the ranks of those world-famous professional artists in all branches who in greater numbers each year make their homes in New York. In return for larger audiences—and salaries—than they can command elsewhere, they have given to the city full measure in setting a high standard of artistic taste.

Andrew Green's dream of a "Greater City" must have been far surpassed on May 26, 1923, when New York opened its Silver Jubilee in the Grand Central Palace. The city, however, was still at its old work of tearing down and rebuilding. The first bronze signal towers for traffic on Fifth Avenue had been unveiled almost at the moment a brass band was rehearsing for the ceremony of demolishing the outworn elevated tracks on upper Sixth Avenue.

If there could have been a kind of super-speed movie projection, like those occasional pictures of the opening of a flower, it would have shown the solid brick, stone and steel of the great city flowing into new forms with every moment.

Buildings, and even districts, would seem to melt away as they were being magically displaced by greater structures.

In 1924, barely three centuries since a few huts had sheltered the beginnings of fur trade on Manhattan Island, the inhabitants of Greater New York were receiving visitors by air. The American-built NC-4 had made its momentous first trans-Atlantic flight from New York to Plymouth, England, and other crossings had followed. In turn, Alcock and Brown, completing the first non-stop flight from England to America, the United States Army round-the-world fliers and the German dirigible, the ZR3 from Friedrichshafen, had alighted to pay their respects to New York City.

One might think that a city accustomed from its earliest infancy to parades, demonstrations and the welcoming of heroes would in time grow blasé, but enthusiasm has never ceased to be the spontaneous expression of New York, where the majority of the population is between the ages of twenty and forty. It is a city of youth.

On June 13, 1927, when Captain Charles A. Lindbergh, United States air mail pilot, came back from his remarkable solo flight across the Atlantic in the "Spirit of St. Louis," there was nothing missing from the reception accorded him—in the avalanche of ticker tape or in the shouting. An escort of ten thousand soldiers preceded him up from the Battery, seven hundred and fifty thousand pounds of torn paper fluttered to the streets, and overhead seventy-five airplanes whirred and swooped and wheeled. To him went the first great, overwhelming welcome for his marvelous feat in aviation, and those who have since followed his daring example have had no cause to complain about the warmth of their greeting. It would be strange, indeed, if a city that literally spends so much of its life hundreds of feet above the earth level were not to a high degree "air-minded."

New York becomes air-minded.

After all, New York may well be characterized as "air-minded" in the sense that no limits are set upon its dreams. Tendencies there are, to be sure: one tendency expressed by the Holland Vehicular Tunnel under the Hudson, completed in 1927; the great Fort Lee Bridge that will span the same river in 1932; in the dedication of the vast medical center uptown; the plans for no less than four new bridges to connect the boroughs to each other and to New Jersey; in prospective tunnels that will serve the same purpose and further speed up vehicular traffic lengthwise in Manhattan—all these and many other projects underscore the tendency of New York toward greater permanence of construction. In the Cathedral of St. John the Divine, soon to be completed as the third largest religious edifice in the world, in the new Temple Emanu-El, the Skyscraper Church, and most definitely in the proposed plan for a great Metropolitan Opera House center, the city shows a conscious growth toward beauty.

There is, moreover, a tendency toward greater preservation of the city's relics of the past. A Museum of the City of New York, the first institution of its kind in any American city, will be completed in the early 1930's, and by reason of a $100,000 gift from the Altman Foundation, will contain a gallery dedicated wholly to Fifth Avenue—that street up which "more famous personages have marched to glory than have done so on any other thoroughfare."

New York's progress from such a recent past to such an amazing present invites at least a guess at its prodigious future.

CHAPTER FORTY-TWO

New York and Tomorrow

THE biography of New York City is a history of constant change. Occupations, dwelling places, manners and customs, and even races have had their brief moment, only to disappear from the city's life or be made over into new forms. Fur-gathering gave way to the bolting and exporting of flour, and that, in turn, was forgotten in the lure of privateering, in the building of the clipper ships and the steamboats, and in the development of great national enterprises. The pointed gables of the Dutch houses fell before the square, white-columned porticos of the English merchants; coffee houses were torn down to make way for granite bank buildings; four stories shot up into ten, then twenty, and presently sixty stories, as if, once freed by the elevator, there could be no limit set upon their number.

No plot of ground has escaped this constant demand of New York that its geographical features, as well as its people, be adaptable. Science has taught the world that the organisms that adapt themselves most readily to new conditions and demands are the ones that best survive; in the intense, vivid life of New York, adaptability has become almost the key-note of success.

The very rapidity with which shafts go down and towers rise suggests a tremendous force that is meant to glory in the *doing* of things as well as in the result. No more striking example of this can be found than in what has taken place on the historic site of The Manhattan Company Building at 40 Wall Street, once the property of the old Dutch governor, Peter Stuyvesant, himself. From the first, progress has placed its varying landmarks here: the famous fence, or "wall," from which Wall Street gained its name, later a large sugar refinery, and then, at the close of the eighteenth century, the handsome three-story mansion of George Scriba.

In the changing conditions that transformed Wall Street from a place of homes to the world's financial center, the Scriba house became, in 1799, the first home of The Manhattan Company. Upon that site, in turn, successive buildings gave way to larger and still larger structures. Then, in 1929, workmen began to demolish most of the lofty buildings covering the entire block bounded by Wall, William, Pine and Nassau Streets. Within thirty days, before many of the offices were even vacated, construction had already begun on the massive foundation of the new Manhattan Company Building and, in less than six months, its framework towered high above the Woolworth Building, long celebrated as the tallest in the world.

Seldom would a citizen recognize the neighborhood in which he carried on his business three or four decades before. That will be truer even of the citizen a decade hence. Just as the textile and the clothing industry migrated uptown from its original home during the early twentieth century, the drug and chemical trades likewise disappeared largely from their first haunts, leaving the old Drug and Chemical Club on John Street to be attended chiefly by insurance men who moved into the district. In the same period most of the hardware trade moved from the vicinity of the City Hall to Lafayette Street and points farther uptown, and the wholesale jewelry trade began to hesitate over the question of abandoning Maiden Lane entirely for its new region in Forty-seventh and Forty-eighth Streets. The paramount financial center has remained in Wall Street, but a new one of large size has developed in the Mid-Manhattan section.

Not less remarkable has been the change in residential sections. It is to be expected that the downtown homes of a century ago would long since have followed the trend uptown, and to suburban districts. But what other city would show so rapid a transformation as is illustrated by one uptown district of Manhattan? Harlem, once Dutch, then English, then native-born American, then largely Jewish, today contains

Old landmarks give way to new on the historic site of
The Manhattan Company Building.

"the largest negro city in the world." So examples could be multiplied: fashionable homes have almost disappeared in Fifth Avenue, below the park, before the march of business; but now Park Avenue is taking its place as the haunt of the wealthy; while newly fashionable districts are being established in regions, once poor, along the East River. As more and more firms and organizations come to establish national headquarters in Manhattan, it may be that dwellings will be pushed farther and farther into the roomy spaces of the other boroughs, and the island will emerge as the office of a nation.

To make a prediction for a Dutch fur-trading post that changed itself in less than three hundred years into a metropolis of over six million people, who use more electricity than all of their Dutch relatives in the Netherlands combined use today, who spend over two million dollars a day on new buildings, and whose incomes pay one-fourth of the tax collected from the whole United States—to predict the future of such a city is no easy task.

One by one, since the days of Hendrik Hudson, "passageways" of commerce have contributed to New York's growth—ocean, river and canal, rail, bridge and tunnel. It may be that the air, into which the Greater New York towers have pierced so far already, holds yet another promise for the City of Tomorrow.

[216]

New York gives little time to thinking of its past. Its concern is with the future. There are those who worry about it. Where, with increasing population, will there be room for people to work, and how will they be transported? If a row of skyscrapers were suddenly to eject all their occupants, the street could not hold them. The volume of shipping is constantly increasing. Where will the ships be moored? The terminals of railroads are already congested. How will a yet greater city be fed, or how will the enormous volume of production that is being constantly supplied, be distributed?

On paper, these may seem to be formidable problems, yet they trouble New York not at all. The solution lies in the rugged confidences, the inspired imagination and the practical common sense which has always distinguished its leaders.

To adjust itself to a population of many millions more, New York is thinking of itself as a greater unit—a new conception of a city which disregards political limits in territory. A recent commission has placed on the map one leg of the compass of this new city at City Hall, and the other fifty miles distant, to include an area of more than three hundred square miles. It is significant that although the need of adjustment to commercial expansion inspired the establishment of the commission, it has provided liberally for parks and parkways, to the end that the new city be not merely big, but comfortable and healthful to live in. Adjustment for increased population and production, therefore, is not its real problem, as New York sees it. Not accommodation of numbers only, but improvement of living standards, are no less pressing requirements. A better governed city, a healthier city, a more beautiful city, a city whose people will be a happier people—these are the objects of the city's dreams and ambitions. To realize these dreams, no class of citizens has been more generous in time, thought and money than the leaders in the commercial world.

It is not that New York is badly governed, or ugly, or unhealthful; not that its people are unhappy. But New York is not satisfied, nor can it ever be satisfied with things as they are. New political and social conditions permit no time for complacency. As the city extends its area and modifies its commercial facilities, it is considering these other demands with quite as much care and attention.

New York serves the nation as commerce serves production and consumption,—not of goods only, but of ideas and ideals. To give this service, it continues to change and improve. The New York that the typical New Yorker visions, will never be, for each present day is but a preparation for the morrow.

CHRONOLOGY

Important Events in the History of New York

The capture of Constantinople by the Turks makes it **1453** necessary for the merchants of Europe to find new routes for commerce to the Orient.

Christopher Columbus opens up the Continent of North **1492** America by his voyage of discovery.

John and Sebastian Cabot explore along the coast of North **1497** America, giving England its first claim to the region about New York.

Giovanni da Verrazzano makes what is probably the first **1524** exploration of the lower bay of New York.

A map of Verrazzano's discoveries is made by his brother, **1529** Girolamo, giving later explorers the idea that a "Sea of Verrazzano" lay beyond New York harbor.

The States General of Hoiland offer a reward of 25,000 **1596** florins for the discovery of a northerly route to the Orient.

James I of England makes a grant to the Plymouth Com- **1606** pany of land in North America including the territory of New York.

Captain Hendrik Hudson, an Englishman in the employ **1609** of the Dutch East India Company, sails into New York harbor and explores the Hudson River as far as its confluence with the Mohawk, seeking a passage to the Orient, via the supposed "Sea of Verrazzano."

The first voyage to the region about the Hudson River for **1610** the purpose of trading is made by a Dutch ship, probably commanded by Hudson's former mate.

1611   Hudson, embarked on another voyage of exploration, is set adrift by his mutinous sailors, to perish on the waters of Hudson's Bay.

1613   The first recorded shipbuilding takes place in the territory now New York, when a Dutch merchant, Captain Block, builds the "Onrust" to replace his vessel, the "Tiger," which had burned.

1614   Exploration of Long Island Sound by Captain Block results in the naming of "New Netherland" (the region about the Hudson River) and of Block Island.

The Dutch New Netherland Company is chartered to trade in this vaguely defined wilderness, under the direction of Hendrick Christiaensen.

A first white child, Jean Vigne, is reputed to have been born in the New Netherland trading-post.

1618   The charter of the New Netherland Company expires, and trade with the newly discovered territory is opened to all Dutch merchants.

1620   The "Mayflower" sails for Manhattan Island, but is prevented from landing here, probably through Dutch trickery, and lands instead at Plymouth Rock.

1621   The Dutch West India Company is chartered by the States General of Holland for twenty-four years, during which time it is to have exclusive rights of trade and government in New Netherland.

1624   The first colonists, thirty families of Walloons, or Belgian Calvinists, arrive at New Netherland under Captain Cornelis May.

1625   Walter Verhulst is appointed director of the Dutch colony.

1626   "Manna-hatin" (so-called in the log of the "Half Moon") is purchased from the Indians for the West India Company by Peter Minuit, newly appointed director of the colony in New Netherland.

Fort New Amsterdam is established at about 1 Broadway, giving its name to the settlement on lower Manhattan.

Reverend Jonas Michaelius is appointed the first dominie *1628* of the Dutch Church at New Amsterdam.

The Dutch West India Company establishes the so-called "patroon system" by which feudal rights are given wealthy merchants who send out to New Netherland fifty colonists at their own expense.

Staten Island is first purchased from the Indians and a *1630* settlement started there.

Wouter van Twiller becomes director of New Netherland, *1633* and brings from Holland Adam Roelantsen, the first school teacher, and the first garrison of one hundred soldiers for Fort New Amsterdam.

The first church building is erected on Manhattan for Dominie Bogardus, the second pastor at New Amsterdam.

King Charles I of England grants Long Island to Alex- *1635* ander, Lord Stirling.

Doctor de la Montagne takes up land as the first white *1636* settler in the region of Yorkville.

Jacques Bentyn and Adrianse Bennett make the first purchase of land at Gowanus, the first step in the evolution of Brooklyn.

Joris de Rapaelje, one of the original Walloon immi- *1637* grants, settles at Wallabout (between Nostrand Avenue and Grand Avenue, Brooklyn). His daughter, Sarah, born about 1624, is reputed to have been the first white girl born in the colony.

William Kieft comes as director of New Netherland. *1638*

The first ferry is established between Manhattan and Long Island, from the present Dover Street, at the corner of Pearl, to Fulton Street, Brooklyn. Cornelis Dircksen is the first ferryman.

The earliest city ordinance is passed, prohibiting private trade in furs, regulating shipping in the port, establishing court days, etc.

Jansen van Vaas is granted land on Long Island, at the site of New Utrecht and Gravesend (now parts of Brooklyn).

1639 Jonas Bronck purchases land in the present Borough of the Bronx (so-called from "Bronck's Land").

1640 The land comprising the present Kings County (Brooklyn) is purchased from the Indians.

A flag signal system is instituted by Patroon Melyn on Staten Island to warn New Amsterdam of incoming ships.

Troubles with the Indians lead to the selection of a committee of twelve representative colonists to advise the director.

1642 Director Kieft dissolves the Committee of Twelve because of their suggestions for reform in the government of the colony.

The City Tavern is erected at about 73 Pearl Street.

The Church of St. Nicholas is built within the fort, the ancestor of the Church of St. Nicholas at Fifth Avenue and Forty-eighth Street.

1643 Disastrous Indian wars that last through 1645 break out in New Netherland.

A council of eight is called by Governor Kieft to advise about the Indian situation.

1644 A fence, referred to as "the wall," is built along the northern limit of the settlement on Manhattan, to keep out cattle. From this the street that later grew up on its site became known as "Wall Street."

Chronology

Vlissingen (Flushing, Long Island) is established by John *1645*
Townsend, Thomas Stiles, and their associates.

The town of Breuckelen (Brooklyn) is established. *1646*
Adrian Van der Donck buys land in the upper West Bronx
Borough, giving it the title Yonkers from "der Jonk-
heer's Landt," (or the Young Lord's Land).

Peter Stuyvesant, sometimes known as "Old Silver Nails," *1647*
because of his silver-banded wooden leg, comes to New
Amsterdam as director of the New Netherland Colony.
An ordinance is passed creating a council of nine men as
part of the government of New Netherland.

The council of nine men, under Adrian Van der Donck, *1649*
sends a document entitled "A Representation of New
Netherlands" to the States General in Holland, protesting
against poor government under the West India Company.

Stuyvesant purchases the great "bouwerie," or farm, on *1651*
Manhattan, from which "The Bowery" is named.
Midwout (Flatbush) is established.

The first city ordinance against fast driving is posted in *1652*
New Amsterdam.
A stockade, or fortification, is built in place of the original
fence along the site of Wall Street.

Civic government is instituted at New Amsterdam by the *1653*
States General, providing for a schout (mayor), two burgo-
masters (aldermen) and five schepens (councillors). The
City Tavern becomes the Stadt Huys, or City Hall.
A first house for the poor is established in Beaver Street.
The city limits of New Amsterdam are set at the Collect
or Fresh Pond (site of the Tombs).
Adrian Van der Donck returns to New Amsterdam from
Holland with a degree and becomes the first lawyer in
the colony.

1654 Breuckelen (Brooklyn) is given city government.

Cromwell makes plans to capture New Amsterdam, and the stockade along Wall Street is strengthened for defensive purposes.

A seal and coat of arms for the city of New Amsterdam and province of New Netherland arrive from Holland.

The first shipload of Jews, twenty-three in number, arrive from Holland under Asser Levy.

1655 The first church on Long Island (Dutch Reformed) is built at Flatbush.

Indian massacres that lay waste Staten Island and parts of Jersey follow the murder of an Indian woman by an official of New Amsterdam.

1656 A charter is issued for Rustdorp (Jamaica).

The first fire wardens are appointed to inspect chimneys in New Amsterdam.

1657 New Utrecht (now a part of Brooklyn) is established.

The Jews are given citizenship rights.

1658 Stuyvesant builds the house later called Whitehall, which gave its name to Whitehall Street.

The village of New Harlem (upper Manhattan) is established by Stuyvesant to encourage agriculture.

A "rattle-watch" is instituted in New Amsterdam to patrol the streets at night, the first city police.

1659 The first kermis, or fair, is held in New Amsterdam.

Alexander Curtius opens the first Latin school on the site of the present 26 Broad Street.

1660 A chapel is erected by Stuyvesant on the site of St-Marks-in-the Bowery.

Dominie Selyns is appointed the first clergyman in the town of Breuckelen.

Chronology

The first post office on Manhattan is opened in the fort.

Between 1660 and 1662, Flushing, Long Island City, Newtown and Hempstead receive charters from Governor Stuyvesant.

The first ferry is established between Manhattan and New 1661 Jersey at Bergen.

The Bowne House (still standing) is erected in Flushing. Here many of the earliest meetings of the persecuted Quakers were held until Stuyvesant banished its owner to Holland.

Delegates from all parts of New Netherland meet in New 1663 Amsterdam and send a remonstrance to Holland, asking that its boundaries be settled and protection afforded.

The States General of Holland give the first official recog- 1664 nition of Dutch rights in New Netherland.

Charles II of England, maintaining English claims over the Dutch territory, bestows it upon his brother, the Duke of York and Albany.

September 6, the forces of James, Duke of York, under Colonel Richard Nicolls, capture the disputed territory.

New Amsterdam becomes New York, and the river known earlier as the Mauritius (in honor of Prince Maurice of Orange) or the North River (to distinguish it from the South or Delaware River) is now called the Hudson River.

Colonel Nicolls is appointed the first English governor of the Province of New York.

The first directory of New York, entitled "List of the 1665 Burghers and Inhabitants of this City That are Assessed for the Lodging of English Soldiers," is made.

A new form of municipal government with a mayor, aldermen and sheriff is established in New York.

Thomas Willett is appointed the first mayor.

The first trial by jury is held in New York.

1666 The first financial "corner" is made in Wall Street: a corner
in wampum, by Frederick Phillipse, one of the dwellers
in the thoroughfare that had grown up along "the wall"
(sometimes called "Cingle Street"). He creates a shortage
by burying several hogsheads of wampum so that those
who had contracted to pay for merchandise in that
medium are forced to purchase it from him at a high rate.

1667 The first public well is dug in New York, within the fort.
By the Treaty of Breda the Dutch cede New York to the
English in exchange for the unimportant little colony of
Surinam in South America.

1668 The Billop House (still standing) is built on Staten Island.
It later becomes the scene of the first peace negotiations
during the American Revolution.
Francis Lovelace succeeds Colonel Nicolls as governor
of the Province of New York.

1670 The first printed description of New York in English is
published in London: "A Brief Description of New York,
Formerly Called New Netherlands," by Daniel Denton.
The first Merchants' Exchange is established by Governor
Lovelace, meeting at Broad Street and Exchange Place.
Staten Island is purchased for the sixth and last time from
the Indians. About this time Captain Charles Billop
saves the island for the Province of New York, by circum-
navigating it within twenty-four hours, the condition upon
which the islands in the bay are allotted to New York
rather than to New Jersey.
Isaac Bedloe is given a grant to "Oyster Island," which
later takes his name.

1672 Peter Stuyvesant dies and is buried in the chapel on the
site of St.-Marks-in-the-Bowery.

1673 Real estate deeds are recorded for the first time in the
city of New York.

Postal service is established between New York and
Boston.

August 9, New York is captured by the Dutch and its
name changed to New Orange. Captain Anthony Colvé
becomes governor.

The Treaty of Westminster restores New York to the *1674*
English; its name is again made New York, and Major
Edmund Andros is sent as governor.

English is adopted as the language of all court records.

The canal that formerly ran down the middle of Broad *1676*
Street is filled in.

The Reverend Charles Wooley comes as the first minister *1678*
of the Church of England.

A "Bolting Act" is passed by the governor and his council, *1680*
giving New York the monopoly of bolting and exporting
flour, and thereby trebling its size and wealth in the next
sixteen years.

The Jews acquire land for a cemetery still existing near *1682*
Chatham Square, the oldest burying ground on Manhattan Island.

A great assembly is held in New York of delegates from *1683*
the entire province, which results in the "Charter of
Liberties and Privileges," outlining a new scheme of
colonial government.

Colonel Thomas Dongan arrives as the new governor of
the province.

The province is divided into counties which are given the
following names: Kings, Queens, Suffolk, Dutchess,
Richmond, New York, Orange, Ulster, Albany, Westchester, Dukes and Cornwall.

A charter is given the City of New York, dividing it into
six wards.

1684　The first common council of the City of New York is sworn into office.

1686　A new seal is adopted for the City of New York.

1688　The Huguenots establish a first French church on the present site of the Produce Exchange.

The government of New York is arbitrarily changed by King James II. It is combined with New England and Edmund Andros is made governor of the entire province.

The seal of New York is destroyed and all previously granted rights and charters declared void.

1689　Upon the accession of William and Mary to the throne of England the Leisler Rebellion occurs in New York City, by which Jacob Leisler, a captain of the city militia, assumes the dictatorship.

Leisler conducts the first popular election in New York and Peter Delanoy is chosen mayor.

1691　With the arrival of Henry Sloughter, the new governor of New York, the Leisler Rebellion is ended, and Jacob Leisler is executed.

The constitutional assembly dissolved by James II is given back to the people of New York by King William and Queen Mary.

The first post-mortem is held in New York, to discover the cause of the sudden death of Governor Sloughter.

1692　King Street (later called Pine) is laid out.

Governor Benjamin Fletcher arrives to rule New York.

1693　William Bradford comes to New York and becomes the first public printer.

The first King's Bridge, giving its name to a later roadway in the Bronx, is built by Frederick Phillipse.

The name of Long Island is changed to Nassau Island.

Chronology

New York laws are printed for the first time, by Bradford. *1694*
The "Bolting Act" is repealed, removing the monopoly
on bolting and exporting flour from New York.
The Quaker meeting house in Flushing (still standing as
the oldest in the country) is built.

Articles of agreement are drawn up between Captain *1695*
Kidd, a merchant of New York, and the Earl of Bellomont,
by which the former is to command the galley "Adventure," sent out in pursuit of pirates.

The first hackney coach appears in New York. *1696*
Captain Kidd assists in the building of the first Trinity
Church on its present site.

The first street lights (lanterns on every seventh house) *1697*
are instituted.
The first public library is sent over by Bishop Compton
of London, for Trinity Church.

The first Trinity Church is completed, with Reverend *1698*
William Vesey, for whom Vesey Street is named, as the
first pastor.
The Earl of Bellomont arrives to succeed Fletcher as
governor of New York.
Quakers are permitted to open a church on Manhattan.

The first license for a theatrical performance is issued in *1699*
New York to Richard Hunter.
Captain Kidd lands on Gardiner's Island, is decoyed to
Boston by Bellomont, and sent captive to London to
answer the charge of piracy.

The title to property now part of Van Cortlandt Park *1701*
is acquired by Jacobus Van Cortlandt.
Captain Kidd is executed in London.
The Earl of Bellomont dies. His remains now lie in St.
Paul's churchyard.

1702 Edward, Lord Cornbury, arrives as governor and the first "freedom of the city" is extended to him.

1703 The Queen's Farm, comprising a vast tract of land from Fulton to Charlton Street, and west from Broadway to the Hudson River, is granted to Trinity Church.
A battery is erected on the point of rocks now filled in and forming the site of the Aquarium at the Battery.

1704 A new City Hall is completed on Wall Street (later converted into Federal Hall).

1708 Lord Lovelace succeeds Lord Cornbury as governor.

1709 The Wall Street Slave Market is established. Later slave entertainments held here originated the modern minstrels.

1710 Trinity School is established.
Three thousand German war refugees arrive from the Palatine, under the protection of Queen Anne, to increase New York's population by 10 per cent.
Robert Hunter arrives to succeed Governor Lovelace.

1713 The first ferry is established between Manhattan and Staten Island.

1714 The first play is published in New York: "Androboros," by Governor Hunter.

1716 Bowery Lane is used for a race course.

1720 William Burnet arrives to succeed Governor Hunter.

1723 Benjamin Franklin, aged seventeen, comes from Philadelphia and pays his first visit to New York.

1725 William Bradford begins the publication of the first New York newspaper, "The New York Gazette," on the present site of the Cotton Exchange.

The first historical work is published in New York: the *1727* volume entitled "A History of the Five Indian Nations," by Cadwallader Colden.

Sir John Montgomerie succeeds Governor Burnet. *1728*

The Merchants' Coffee House is erected at the corner of Wall and Water Streets on the site of the later Tontine Coffee House.

Colonel Abraham de Peyster dies and his will provides for a bell to be cast in Holland for the Dutch Reformed Church then being built in Nassau Street. (This bell is now in the belfry of the Church of St. Nicholas at Fifth Avenue and Forty-eighth Street.)

The first Jewish Synagogue, the Shearith Israel, is com- *1729* pleted in Mill Street.

Cherry Street is laid out and named for the cherry orchard *1730* of Richard Sackett.

Frankfort Street is named in honor of Jacob Leisler's birthplace in Germany.

A new city charter is granted by Governor Montgomerie *1731* dividing the city into seven wards and taking in the village of Harlem.

The city issues its first municipal bonds.

Colonel William Cosby arrives to succeed Governor *1732* Montgomerie.

The first theatre, probably on Maiden Lane and Pearl Street, opens with a comedy, "The Recruiting Officer."

The common council leases the plain at the foot of Broad- *1733* way to John Chambers, Peter Bayard, and Peter Jay for one peppercorn a year, on condition that they maintain it as a bowling green, thus giving it its present name of Bowling Green.

The second New York newspaper, "The New York Weekly Journal," is begun by John Peter Zenger and becomes the spokesman for the "masses."

1735 Zenger is tried for libel and his acquittal establishes freedom of the press.

1739 Greenwich Street is surveyed and laid out.

1740 The first record is kept of naturalized citizens of New York.

1741 A supposed plot to burn the city leads to a brief reign of terror and wholesale executions.

1743 George Clinton arrives to be governor of New York.

1744 The first afternoon paper, the first newspaper established by a native New Yorker, is begun by Henry de Forest, the "New York Evening Post" (not the present publication of that name).

1745 Land in the region of the present Abingdon Square, Greenwich, is granted to Sir Peter Warren. The square takes its name at a later period from Sir Warren's daughter, Lady Abingdon.

1750 Captain Thomas Clark buys land north of Greenwich Village, extending from Eighth Avenue to the Hudson River and from Nineteenth to Twenty-fourth Street, to which the name Chelsea is given by him.

1753 The famous Hallam family of actors come to New York and give their first performance, a production of "The Conscious Lovers."
Sir Danvers Osborn succeeds Governor Clinton.

1754 King's College is chartered, with Dr. Samuel Johnson, of Stratford, Connecticut, as first president. Its first building is erected near the present site of the Woolworth Building.

Chronology

The first quarantine station for incoming ships is estab- *1755* lished at Bedloe's Island.

The present Park Row is laid out.

Sir Charles Hardy arrives to be governor.

The Scotch Presbyterian Church is formed and opens a *1756* place of worship on Cedar Street between Broadway and Nassau Street.

Colonel George Washington of Virginia pays his first visit to New York

The library of King's College is founded by a bequest of *1757* Joseph Murray, winner of the first prize in a lottery opened to raise money for the establishment of the college.

The city buys Bedloe's Island, then called Kennedy's. *1758* King's College holds its first commencement.

The first Baptist meeting house is completed at the present *1760* 35-42 Gold Street.

The first free school is opened for negroes.

A second bridge is built over the Harlem River.

The first monument in New York is erected for General *1761* Wolfe, hero of the French and Canadian Wars, at Sixth Avenue and Fourteenth Street.

Sir Jeffrey Amherst, for whom Amherst College is named, is made Knight of the Bath at ceremonies on Staten Island, the first investiture of orders in America.

Samuel Fraunces buys Etienne de Lancey's house at the *1762* corner of Pearl and Broad Streets, making it over into Fraunces' Tavern.

Major-General Robert Monckton arrives to be governor.

The Society for the Promotion of Arts, Agriculture and *1764* Economy in the Province of New York is founded at Fraunces' Tavern.

1765 The Stamp Act Congress meets in Wall Street, a merchants' protest against the English Stamp Act.
The Sons of Liberty are organized in New York.
Sir Henry Moore arrives to be governor.

1766 The Roger Morris House, now known as the Jumel Museum, is erected at the present 161st Street and St. Nicholas Ave.
The Stamp Act is repealed and a flagstaff called a "liberty pole" is erected on the Common (City Hall Park) in celebration of the colony's triumph.
The Mutiny Act, quartering British soldiers in New York at the city's expense, is passed by Parliament.
St. Paul's Chapel is completed and dedicated.

1767 A first Methodist meeting house is established in John Street and built through the assistance of all other denominations then existing in the city.

1768 The New York Chamber of Commerce is organized.
The New York merchants draw up a non-importation agreement in protest against the Townshend Acts, which provided for a tax on various articles of import.

1769 Milestones are placed from the City Hall on Wall Street along Kingsbridge Road (so called because it led from lower Manhattan to the King's Bridge).

1770 The Battle of Golden Hill (at the present John Street) occurs, the first "battle" of the Revolution with bloodshed on both sides, between the townspeople and the garrison soldiers.
Walter Franklin's house at 3 Cherry Street is erected, later to become the first "White House" of the nation.
The Earl of Dunmore arrives to succeed Moore as governor.

1771 William Tryon is made governor.

Chronology

The New York "tea party" occurs: a protest against 1774
Parliament's tax on tea. The citizens force the captain
to turn about his ship bearing his cargo of tea and return
to England.

A committee is formed in New York to correspond with
other colonies on the subject of colonial grievances. New
York sends delegates to the first Continental Congress,
among them John Jay, who makes the first draft of the
Declaration of Independence.

The New York Committee of Safety is established, often 1775
making its headquarters during the Revolution at the
Christopher House still standing on Staten Island.

The first New York hospital is erected on the site of 319 1776
Broadway.

The Continental Congress drafts the Articles of Confederation.

General Washington comes to New York as Commander-
in-Chief of the Colonial Army.

General Howe makes the first attempt at peace negotiations in the Billop House on Staten Island.

The Battle of Long Island, fought at Jamaica Pass on the
Flatbush Road, at the site of the Greenwood Cemetery,
and at a point near the present junction of Tenth Street
and Fifth Avenue in Brooklyn, results in a crushing defeat
for the American forces.

General Washington effects a masterly retreat from Brooklyn Heights to Manhattan.

The British General, Howe, lands at Kips Bay on the
East River, routing its American defenders, who retreat
across the Murray Hill section. Following this, General
Howe is detained at luncheon by Mrs. Murray so that
the American forces are enabled to concentrate their
strength in northern Manhattan.

Nathan Hale is captured by the British in New York and
hanged as a spy near the northwest corner of Third
Avenue and Sixty-sixth Street.

The British take possession of New York City.

A disastrous fire destroys a great number of buildings in the city, among them Trinity Church.

The Battle of Harlem Heights (including the site of the present Columbia University Campus) results in a defeat for the British.

Fort Washington, at West 183rd Street, is captured by the British through the treachery of Adjutant-General William Demont, who furnishes General Howe with plans of the fortress.

New York City becomes a prison headquarters for the duration of the Revolution, the City Hall, an old sugar house on Liberty Street, the Middle Dutch Church at Nassau and Cedar Streets, and prison ships anchored in Wallabout Bay, serving as the most notorious dungeons.

1777 The Provincial Congress of New York meets at Kingston and adopts a state constitution, electing George Clinton, a native of Orange County, New York, and a leader in the struggle for independence, as the first American governor of New York State.

1778 New York State ratifies the Articles of Confederation.

1780 Major-General James Robertson succeeds Tryon as British governor of New York.

The treason of Benedict Arnold is discovered and he flees from West Point to New York City.

1781 Fort George is erected on the present site of the George Washington High School.

The first visit is paid to New York by a Prince of Wales, the future William IV.

1782 The Prince of Wales is made a Knight of the Garter by ceremonies held in New York.

1783 The British evacuate New York.

Chronology

General Washington delivers his famous farewell address to his officers at Fraunces' Tavern.

Between twelve and fifteen thousand English loyalists depart from New York and their estates are confiscated by the new government.

The present seal of the City of New York is adopted.   *1784*
Catholicism is established in New York by Father Farmer.
New York City becomes the capital of the state, and the State Legislature meets here, until 1798.
James Duane is named by the governor of the state as the first mayor of New York City under American rule.
The "Empress of China," owned by New York merchants, makes first commercial voyage from New York to Asia.
The name of King's College is changed to Columbia College.

The Continental Congress establishes New York as its   *1785*
meeting place, and continues to meet here until 1788.
William Morton and Samuel Horner establish the first New York daily paper, "The New York Morning Post and Daily Advertiser."
The General Society of Mechanics and Tradesmen is established.

John Pintard establishes the first successful fire insurance   *1786*
company, the Mutual Assurance.
The Chamber of Commerce endorses the Erie Canal project, first suggested by Christopher Colles.

Erasmus Hall Academy is established in Flatbush.   *1787*
The Reverend Samuel Provoost becomes the first Protestant Episcopal Bishop of New York.
The "Federalist" essays of Alexander Hamilton, James Madison and John Jay are published in New York, advocating a more centralized form of national government.
Noah Webster establishes a first magazine in New York

under the name "American Magazine" (not to be confused with the present publication of that name).

1788   The "doctors' riot" occurs, an outburst of popular superstition against the dissecting of corpses.

The City Hall on Wall Street is remodeled into Federal Hall and becomes the first meeting place of Congress.

A mammoth parade on behalf of the Federal Constitution is held in New York and encourages its ratification by New York State.

1789   George Washington takes the oath of office as first President of the United States in Federal Hall, at the corner of Wall and Nassau Streets, an event commemorated by his statue on the steps of the present Sub-Treasury Building.

Alexander Hamilton, a resident of New York City, is appointed the first Secretary of the Treasury of the United States by President Washington.

St. Tammany's Society (Tammany Hall) is formed.

John Jay, a citizen of New York, is appointed the first Chief Justice of the United States and convenes the first session of the Supreme Court of the United States in New York City.

The first American Museum, later to become famous as Barnum's Museum, is founded by the Tammany Society.

The Stock Exchange is formed by a dozen merchants meeting under a buttonwood tree at 68 Wall Street.

Richard Varick is appointed mayor of New York.

1790   The second Trinity Church edifice is dedicated.

1792   A first medical school is established at Columbia College under Dr. Samuel Bard.

Gilbert Stuart comes to paint portraits in New York.

1793   James Kent institutes a college of law at Columbia College.

The city purchases "Belle Vue," the estate of Brockholst *1794*
Livingston, the location for the present Bellevue Hospital.

The Gracie Mansion, later made the first home of the
Museum of the City of New York, on East Eighty-ninth
Street, is erected.

John Butler founds the Unitarian Church in New York.

"Tammany, or the Indian Chief," the first opera written
and produced in America is given in New York.

The Tontine Coffee House, long famous as a meeting
place for merchants, is completed at Wall and Water
Streets.

The land now comprising Madison Square is acquired by
the city and set apart as a burial ground.

John Jay, sent as Minister Plenipotentiary to Great *1795*
Britain, returns with his famous commercial treaty between the United States and England, which greatly increases the prosperity of New York merchants.

John Fitch experiments with a partially successful steam- *1796*
boat of his own invention, on the Collect Pond.

James Oram begins the "New York Prices Current,"
later the "New York Commercial" (now merged with the
"New York Journal of Commerce").

The "Betsey," built in New York in 1792, carries the *1797*
Stars and Stripes for the first time around the world.

Washington Square is purchased by the city for a paupers'
burial ground.

The city charter is amended to provide for the appointment
of the mayor and other charter officers by the governor
of the state and a council of appointments.

The Park Theatre, famous for fifty years, is opened in *1798*
Park Row, between Ann and Beekman Streets, with a
performance of "As You Like It."

A yellow fever epidemic sweeps the city.

1799 The first Long Island newspaper is founded by Thomas Kirk—"The Courier and New York and Long Island Advertiser."

A corporation entitled "The President and Directors of the Manhattan Company" is chartered as the first public utility of New York, a water company with a clause written into its charter by Aaron Burr that permitted it to open a bank, now known as the Bank of Manhattan Trust Company.

Daniel Ludlow is elected the first president of the Manhattan Company and Henry Remsen the first cashier of the Company's bank, opened at 40 Wall Street, the site of its present main office.

The city of New York becomes a shareholder in the Manhattan Company.

The present St.-Marks-in the-Bowery is completed.

1800 Alexander Hamilton erects his home, "The Grange," now standing on Convent Avenue.

Aaron Burr is elected Vice-President of the United States.

Bedloe's, Ellis and Governor's Islands are ceded by New York to the Federal government.

The Manhattan Company declares its first dividend.

1801 Francis Childs and his wife sell the site of the Brooklyn Navy Yard to the government for five dollars.

Captain Robert R. Randall provides by bequest for the founding of Sailors' Snug Harbor now at New Brighton, Staten Island.

Hamilton helps to establish the "New York Evening Post," edited by William Coleman, the oldest daily paper in New York City which has retained its original name.

Edward Livingston is appointed mayor of New York by the governor and council of appointments.

1802 Robert Fulton and Rober Livingston enter into an agreement to experiment with steam navigation.

De Witt Clinton, a nephew of Governor George Clinton, *1803*
is appointed mayor of New York City.

The New York Historical Society is founded. *1804*
The First Congregational Church in New York opens a
place of worship on Warren Street.   . .
Charter amendments extend the franchise to all males
over twenty-one who have established a six months' residence in New York, and who pay a yearly rental of at
least twenty-five dollars.
Alexander Hamilton is killed in a duel fought with Aaron
Burr at Weehawken. He is buried in Trinity churchyard,
where a monument marks his grave.

The Society for the Establishment of a Free School for the *1805*
City of New York is founded.
The New York State Legislature authorizes the establishment of the Merchants' Bank of New York, under a
charter drawn by Alexander Hamilton in 1803.

Marinus Willett is appointed mayor. *1807*
Robert Fulton's steamboat, the "Clermont," makes a first
successful trip from New York to Albany, ushering in
the new era of steam transportation.

De Witt Clinton is again appointed mayor. *1808*
New York City is made an Episcopal See by Pope Pius II.
The charter of the Manhattan Company is amended to
permit the sale of its water works to the city and to enable
the State of New York to purchase 1000 shares for $50,000,
stock which it has continued to hold in perpetuity for the
common school fund.
Henry Remsen is elected president of the Manhattan
Company.

Washington Irving's "Father Knickerbocker's History of *1809*
New York" is published.

Branch offices of the bank of the Manhattan Company are opened at Utica and Poughkeepsie.

Free Public School Number One opens on Chatham Street.

1810 Castle William on Governor's Island is completed, and named for Colonel Jonathan Williams, in charge of defenses of New York harbor.

The Collect, or Fresh Water Pond, on the site of the Tombs, is filled in.

Jacob Radcliff is appointed mayor.

1811 The City Planning Commission completes the "Commissioners' Map" which lays out the present city streets and squares as far north as 155th Street.

The first steam ferry is established to Hoboken.

John Howard Payne, author of "Home, Sweet Home," opens the first public reading room, in the City Hotel at Broadway and Thames Street.

De Witt Clinton is again appointed mayor.

1812 New York completes and dedicates its new City Hall in City Hall Park.

War is declared with Great Britain, and New York has a recurrence of privateering.

1813 The name "The Bowery" is adopted for Bowery Lane.

Captain James Lawrence, author of the words "Don't give up the ship!" is killed in an encounter between the "Chesapeake" and the "Shannon." He is buried with military honors in Trinity churchyard.

1814 The American frigate, "President," runs through the British blockade and protects New York City from British attack.

The first steam frigate, the "Demologos," is launched in the shipyard of Adam and Noah Brown at Corlears Hook.

Citizens of New York and surrounding towns volunteer to build defenses, among them Fort Clinton still standing at McGowan's Pass.

The first Board of Health is established. **1815**
John Ferguson serves for three months as mayor and is succeeded by Jacob Radcliff, again appointed to the office.

Sugarloaf Street is renamed Franklin Street for Benjamin **1816** Franklin.

An act is passed to free all slaves in New York State by **1817** 1827.
De Witt Clinton is elected governor of New York State.

Clement C. Moore, author of " 'Twas the Night Before **1818** Christmas," gives to the General Theological Seminary ground it now occupies on Ninth Avenue.
Cadwallader Colden is appointed mayor of New York.
The Manhattan Company is designated Transfer Agent for the State of New York, in which capacity it has served continuously to the present time.

The first velocipede appears in New York. **1819**
The "Savannah" sails from New York to England on the first trans-Atlantic voyage under steam.
Canal Street is completed.
The branch banks of the Manhattan Company in Utica and Poughkeepsie are discontinued.

A first Court of Common Pleas is established in New York. **1821**
A charter amendment provides for the appointment of the mayor by the city council, and Stephen Allen is the first mayor so appointed.

Fulton Market is established. **1822**
Congress cedes to the city the Battery and Castle Clinton,

so-called for De Witt Clinton (later Castle Garden), the site of the present Aquarium.

1823 The present Bryant Park is acquired by the city for a burial ground.

1824 The Marquis de Lafayette, who served as one of General Washington's aides during the Revolution, revisits America and is enthusiastically welcomed in New York City.

The New York National Guard, later the famous Seventh Regiment, is formed at the Shakespeare Tavern on the northwest corner of Nassau and Fulton Streets.

Fifth Avenue is opened as far north as Thirteenth Street.

A monopoly given to Robert Livingston in 1798 on steam navigation is declared illegal and New York begins to profit from steam transportation.

The Bank of Long Island, the first Brooklyn bank, is incorporated with Leffert Lefferts as president.

1825 The completion of the Erie Canal is celebrated in New York.

The first grand opera is given in New York at the Park Theatre, "The Barber of Seville."

John G. Coster is elected president of the Manhattan Company.

"Slote Lane" is renamed Exchange Street.

William Paulding is appointed mayor.

1826 All property qualifications are removed from voters in New York.

Philip Hone is appointed mayor.

1827 The college known as the Flushing Institute is founded by the Reverend W. A. Muhlenburg. It is later moved to College Point, which takes its name from this fact.

William Paulding is again appointed mayor.

The "Journal of Commerce" is established.

Walter Bowne is appointed mayor of New York.   *1829*
Maltby Gelston becomes president of the Manhattan
Company.

July 27, ground is broken for the Mohawk and Hudson *1830*
Railroad, the first railroad line (now part of the New
York Central). Lynde Catlin, president of the Merchants' Bank (merged in 1920 with the Manhattan Company), is designated a commissioner by the terms of the
railroad company's charter and is later elected director
and first treasurer.

A regular stage line is established on Broadway from
Bowling Green to Bleecker Street.

Samuel Ruggles transforms Gramercy Park into a unique *1831*
private park for the benefit of those owning property surrounding it.

New York University is established.

August 9, the first trip is made over the Mohawk and
Hudson Railroad between Albany and Schenectady.

The New York and Harlem Railroad begins operating *1832*
with horse cars from Prince Street to Murray Hill.

The "New York Morning Post" is established by Horace
Greeley.

The New York and Albany Railroad is incorporated.

The first opera house is built in Church Street.   *1833*
Gideon Lee is appointed mayor.

The "New York Sun" is founded by Benjamin Day.

Daniel Webster visits New York and makes a speech from *1834*
his lodgings in Greenwich Street.

Brooklyn is incorporated as a city, with George Hall as
first mayor under its new charter.

The United States Marine Hospital is established at its
present site on Staten Island.

[245]

Steam trains first appear on the Harlem Railroad.

The charter of New York City is amended to provide for the popular election of the mayor, and Cornelius van Wyck Lawrence is the first executive so elected.

1835   The so-called "Great Fire" breaks out in Hanover and Pearl Streets, destroying nearly 700 buildings, and property to the value of $17,000,000.

James Gordon Bennett establishes the "New York Herald."

The city buys Randall's Island.

1836   The Union Club is founded in New York.

Judges are first elected by popular vote in the city.

1837   A convention of 136 delegates from banks all over the United States meets in New York to consider matters relating to the financial panic of this year.

Martin Van Buren, the first native New Yorker to hold that office, is elected President of the United States.

The first vaudeville show is held at Niblo's Garden, on the east side of Broadway, between Prince and Houston Streets.

Madison Square is laid out as a park.

The New York and Harlem Railroad inaugurates its service as far north as Harlem.

Aaron Clark is elected mayor.

Professor Samuel F. B. Morse of the University of New York invents a practical electric telegraph and transmission code.

1838   Flushing, Long Island, is incorporated as a city.

The first Tombs Prison is completed.

1839   William Harnden inaugurates the first express service between New York and Boston.

Isaac Varian is elected mayor.

The Manhattan Company erects a two-story granite building at 40 Wall Street to replace its original office.

The Cunard Steamship line is established. *1840*
Edgar Allan Poe comes to live in the Fordham Cottage now standing on the Grand Concourse and Kingsbridge Road.
Jonathan Thompson is elected president of the Manhattan Company.

Horace Greeley founds the "New York Tribune." *1841*
The "Brooklyn Eagle" is founded with Isaac Van Arden as first editor.
The Audubon House, still standing at 156th Street and Riverside Drive, is built and occupied by John J. Audubon, author of "Birds of America."
The first screw-propeller vessel, the "Princeton," is built by John Ericsson of New York, whose monument now stands in the Battery.
John W. Griffiths, naval architect of New York, designs the first "clipper ship," destined to inaugurate what is known as the "Golden Age" of New York shipping.
The first steam fire engine is tried in New York.
Robert H. Morris is elected mayor.
The first section of the Erie Railroad is put in operation from New York via Piermont to Goshen.

The Croton water system is completed and its opening *1842* celebrated in New York City.
The Manhattan Company ceases to function as a water company and employs its entire capital in the business of banking.
The New York Philharmonic Society is organized.
Charles Dickens visits New York for the first time.
The celebrated dwarf, Tom Thumb, is exhibited at Barnum's Museum.

1844 James Harper is elected mayor.

1845 A municipal police system is adopted and George W. Watsell is made the first chief of police.

The great national game of baseball is originated by the founding of the Knickerbocker Baseball Club of New York, the first baseball club to be organized in America.

William F. Havemeyer is elected mayor.

1846 The present Trinity Church is dedicated, the third church building on that site.

Elias Howe patents the sewing machine, and his invention has an important effect on the development of the garment industry in New York City.

The United States Government establishes a sub-treasury in New York City.

Fordham University is founded.

Andrew H. Mickle is elected mayor.

1847 The first evening free schools are opened.

The Plymouth Congregational Church of Brooklyn is built.

William B. Brady is elected mayor.

Caleb O. Halsted is elected president of the Manhattan Company.

1848 The New York newspapers join with the Telegraph Company to establish the Associated Press.

The Park Theatre is destroyed by fire.

The first prisoners are sent to Blackwell's Island (now Welfare Island).

William F. Havemeyer is again elected mayor.

The Manhattan Company enlarges its office building at 40 Wall Street by adding a third story and extending the edifice over the vacant lot in the rear.

1849 The New York Free Academy is founded.

Caleb S. Woodhull is elected mayor.

A charter amendment increases the mayor's term of office from one to two years.

The Astor Place Riot occurs with much bloodshed as a result of the quarrel between William C. Macready, an English actor, and Edwin Forrest, an American actor.

The first elevator is installed at 201-203 Cherry Street. *1850*
"Harper's Weekly" is founded.

The exiled General Garibaldi comes to make his home on Staten Island for several months.

P. T. Barnum introduces Jenny Lind at Castle Garden in a series of concerts.

The celebrated clipper ship, "Flying Cloud," built by *1851*
Donald McKay of Boston, and owned by New York merchants, makes a record trip between New York and San Francisco in eighty-nine days and eighteen hours.

The Hudson River Railroad is opened, from New York to Albany.

Louis Kossuth, the Hungarian patriot, is welcomed to New York.

Henry J. Raymond founds the "New York Times."

Ambrose C. Kingsland is elected mayor.

The American Geographical Society is founded in New *1852*
York City.

William M. Thackeray visits New York.

The city charter is amended, dividing the city into twenty-two wards and creating a board of police commissioners; uniforms are adopted for the police: blue coats with brass buttons and gray trousers.

Adelina Patti makes her debut in New York at the age of eight years.

Jacob A. Westervelt is elected mayor.

The first step is taken toward the consolidation of seven *1853*
separate railroads between Albany and Troy on the east,

and Buffalo and Niagara Falls on the west, into the New York Central Railroad Company.

The Assay Office is established in Wall Street.

A World's Fair is held in New York at the Crystal Palace, on the site of Bryant Park.

"Uncle Tom's Cabin" runs for two hundred consecutive performances at the Chatham Theatre, in Chatham Square.

The Central Park project is authorized, and commissioners are appointed, of whom Andrew H. Green, sponsor of the idea of Greater New York, is later made president.

The Clearing House Association is formed in New York, the Manhattan Company standing second on its roll of membership.

1854 Fernando Wood is elected mayor.

The Packer Institute for Girls is founded in Brooklyn.

The Academy of Music is opened on Fourteenth Street and Irving Place.

1855 Bushwick and Williamsburg are added to Brooklyn.

The Polytechnic Institute for Boys is established in Brooklyn.

Castle Garden becomes an immigrant station.

1856 A bronze statue of Washington is unveiled in Union Square (so-called because it marked the convergence of many streets).

A "slave auction" is held in the Plymouth Congregational Church of Brooklyn as a protest againt slavery by the Reverend Henry Ward Beecher.

Columbia College is moved to Fourth Avenue between Forty-ninth and Fiftieth Streets.

1857 A metropolitan police district (discontinued in 1863), is established, placing the New York City police under state control.

Frederick Law Olmsted and Calvert Vaux win the competition for a plan of development for Central Park. *1858*
Daniel F. Tiemann is elected mayor.
The Crystal Palace is destroyed by fire.
A mammoth celebration of the first laying of the transAtlantic cable by Cyrus W. Field is held in New York.

Voters register for the first time in New York. *1859*
"Dixie" is sung for the first time, from the stage of Bryant's Minstrels at 472 Broadway.
Cooper Union for the Advancement of Science and Art (founded by Peter Cooper in 1857) is established in Astor Place on its present site.

Abraham Lincoln, candidate for the presidency of the *1860* United States, makes his famous speech at Cooper Union which introduces him to New York City.
The "Pony Express" links New York with San Francisco.
Commissioners are appointed to lay out streets north of 155th Street.
The first laws are passed requiring fire escapes on tenement houses.
The Prince of Wales, later King Edward VII, visits New York.
A Japanese Embassy, the first to be sent to this country, arrives in New York.
Fernando Wood is again elected mayor.
James M. Morrison is elected president of the Manhattan Company.

Abraham Lincoln is welcomed, en route to the White *1861* House.
Fort Sumter is captured by the Confederates and the Union flag is saved by Peter Hart, a New York policeman serving under Major Anderson.
The Seventh Regiment of New York (the National Guard) departs for the front under Colonel M. Lefferts.

The Committee of Union Defense is formed in New York under John A. Dix and sends the first ambulances to the seat of war.

A seat on the Stock Exchange is sold for the first time at auction, for $460. (In 1929 the cost had risen to $625,000.)

1862 John Ericsson's ironclad "Monitor," made famous by its engagement with the "Merrimac" during the Civil War, is launched at Greenpoint, Long Island.

The first hansom cab appears on the streets of New York.

George Opdyke is elected mayor.

Delmonico's famous restaurant is opened at Fifth Avenue and Fourteenth Street.

1863 The Sub-Treasury occupies, for the first time, the building at the corner of Wall and Nassau Streets.

The Union League Club is organized at 26 East Seventeenth Street to aid in preserving the Union, and does its first work in recruiting negro troops for the Civil War.

The Draft Riots occur in New York, causing the death of over twelve hundred people.

1864 Charles G. Gunther is elected mayor.

A Metropolitan Fair held in New York nets over a million dollars for the United States Sanitary Commission.

1865 The funeral cortege of Lincoln, en route to Springfield, Illinois, passes through the city, which is placed in deep mourning.

Direct telegraph communication is opened between New York and San Francisco.

The New York metropolitan fire district, including Brooklyn, is created, the end of the old volunteer fire system.

1866 The Free Academy is made the College of the City of New York.

John T. Hoffman is elected mayor.

Chronology

James G. Bennett establishes the "New York Evening *1867*
Telegram," now one of the Scripps-Howard publications.
"Stock tickers" are first introduced.
The plan for West Side development including Riverside
Drive, is adopted by the city.

"Sorosis," the first women's club in New York, is incor- *1868*
porated.
The first experimental elevated railroad is erected from
the Battery to Cortlandt Street on Greenwich Street.
The Beach Pneumatic Transit Company is given a right
to build a subway from Fourteenth Street to Nassau
Street, but the attempt is abandoned.
The New York Athletic Club is organized.
Andrew H. Green of Brooklyn first advocates Greater
New York.

Broadway is laid out as a "boulevard" north of Fifty- *1869*
ninth Street.
The panic of "Black Friday" occurs as a result of an
attempted "corner" of the gold market on the New York
Stock Exchange.
A. Oakey Hall is elected mayor.

The New York Bar Association is organized. *1870*
Work is started on the construction of Brooklyn Bridge.
The Equitable Life Assurance Society Building is erected
on Broadway at Cedar Street, the first office building in
New York equipped with passenger elevators.
Long Island City is incorporated as a city.
An expedition sent by the "New York Herald" under
Henry M. Stanley finds David Livingstone in British
East Africa.

The New York Cotton Exchange is incorporated. *1871*
Steam trains are first used on the elevated railroad in
Greenwich Street.

The "Tweed Ring" of corrupt politicians is overthrown.
The first Grand Central Terminal is completed at Forty-second Street.
Grand Duke Alexis of Russia visits New York.
Chester A. Arthur is appointed collector of the port.

1872 East New York is annexed to Brooklyn.
William F. Havemeyer is again elected mayor.
Forty thousand men are idle as a result of a disastrous general strike of all building trades.

1873 The towns of Kingsbridge, Morrisania and West Farms are added to New York, extending the city limits to Yonkers.
The prison ship martyrs' remains are reburied at Fort Greene, Washington Park, Brooklyn.
The failure of J. Cooke & Company precipitates a panic in Wall Street.

1874 Barnum's Great Roman Hippodrome opens at Twenty-seventh Street and Madison Avenue.
The governments of the city and county are again consolidated.

1875 The Rapid Transit Commission is created.
William H. Wickham is elected mayor.

1876 The first through train runs from New York to San Francisco.
Hell Gate Channel is opened by the blasting of rocks near Hallett's Point.
Central Park is completed.

1877 The first high-wheeled bicycle appears in New York.
Alfred T. White, of Brooklyn, erects the first tenement building around a central court.
Smith Ely is elected mayor.

Chronology

The New York Symphony Society is organized through the *1878*
efforts of Dr. Leopold Damrosch.

The New York Museum of Natural History is opened by
President Hayes.

The first directory of telephones in New York is issued.

Edward Cooper is elected mayor.

St. Patrick's Cathedral (completed in 1910) is dedicated *1879*
by Cardinal McCloskey.

The operetta "Pinafore" is given its premiere in New York
City.

The Republican Club of New York is organized.

The first Madison Square Garden is opened.

J. F. Harberger is elected president of the Manhattan
Company.

The elevated railroad system is completed to the Harlem *1880*
River.

The New York Metropolitan Museum of Art is opened
by President Hayes.

Count Ferdinand de Lesseps, the projector of the Panama
Canal, comes to New York to solicit American capital.

Sarah Bernhardt makes her debut in New York in "Adri-
enne Lecouvreur."

Broadway is electrically lighted for the first time, with
British arc lights.

William H. Smith is elected president of the Manhattan
Company.

William R. Grace is elected mayor of New York. *1881*

Cleopatra's Needle, a gift of the Khedive of Egypt, is presented to New York, its transportation and pedestal in
Central Park paid for by William H. Vanderbilt.

Seth Low is elected mayor of Brooklyn.

The Union League Club moves into its new club house at
Thirty-ninth Street and Fifth Avenue.

The city goes into mourning upon the assassination of President Garfield.

1882 The "New York Morning Journal" is founded by Joseph Pulitzer.

The Edison Company begins operating, inaugurating the first commercial lighting by electricity in New York City.

A group of young men form the City Reform Club at the home of Theodore Roosevelt.

The Metropolitan Opera House at Broadway and Thirty-ninth Street is opened (unfinished) with Strauss' operetta, "The Queen's Lace Handkerchief."

1883 May 24—the Brooklyn Bridge, the longest suspension bridge in the world, is opened.

The New York Telephone and Telegraph Company is incorporated.

Henry Irving and Ellen Terry make their debuts in New York.

The Centennial of the British Evacuation of New York is celebrated, and the statue of Washington on the steps of the Sub-Treasury Building is unveiled.

The Metropolitan Opera House is formally opened with a performance of "Faust."

Franklin Edson is elected mayor.

1884 A long distance telephone is established between New York and Boston.

John Singer Sargent begins making portraits in New York.

The name of "Reservoir Square" at Forty-second Street is changed to Bryant Park.

A new building of the Manhattan Company, erected jointly with the Merchants' Bank, is completed at 40-42 Wall Street. D. C. Hayes is elected president of the Manhattan Company.

Leopold Damrosch inaugurates the first season of German opera in New York.

The failures of Keene, of the Marine Bank, and the firm of Grant & Ward all help to precipitate a financial panic.

The first cable cars are operated on Amsterdam Avenue.   *1885*
The first law is passed regulating the height of buildings in New York
General Grant dies in New York City, and a funeral procession six miles in length escorts his body to the temporary tomb on the site of the present Grant's Tomb on Riverside Drive.
The Fifth Avenue Bus Line is inaugurated.
The Statue of Liberty is unveiled, a gift to the United States from the people of France.
William R. Grace is again elected mayor.

Joseph Pulitzer founds the "New York Evening World." *1887*
Charles A. Dana founds the "New York Evening Sun."
Electric street cars are used for the first time.
Abram S. Hewitt is elected mayor.

The "Great Blizzard" occurs, raging for three days and *1888*
covering New York with twenty-two inches of snow.
The first modern "steel skeleton" structure is erected, the Tower Building at 50 Broadway.
The Fulton Street elevated line is completed in Brooklyn.
Electric trains are installed for the first time on the New York elevated railway lines.

The Centennial of Washington's Inauguration is cele- *1889*
brated in New York. A temporary arch, later made permanent, is erected in Washington Square, the designer Stanford White.
Hugh J. Grant is elected mayor.

Coney Island is annexed to Brooklyn.   *1890*
General Charles Sooey Smith invents the caisson form of

construction for foundations of skyscrapers, greatly affecting the architecture of New York.

A second Madison Square Garden, designed by Stanford White, is opened.

The U. S. S. "Maine" is launched at the Brooklyn Navy Yard, destined to precipitate a war between the United States and Spain by its sinking in the Harbor of Havana, Cuba, in 1898.

1891 The Botanical Gardens are opened at Bronx Park.

"The Old Homestead" completes a three-year run at the Academy of Music.

The first four-track bridge is completed over the Harlem River, the steel bridge of the Harlem and New Haven line.

Carnegie Hall, the gift of Andrew Carnegie, is opened.

1892 The cornerstone of the Cathedral of St. John the Divine on Morningside Heights, is laid.

Ellis Island is established as an immigrant station.

A Columbus celebration is held, during which the Columbus Monument at Fifty-ninth Street is presented to New York by its Italian citizens.

The first building of the Metropolitan Opera House burns.

The Manhattan Opera House, under the management of Oscar Hammerstein, is opened.

Mrs. Astor gives her celebrated ball at the Astor Hotel, originating the term "The Four Hundred."

The Reverend Dr. Parkhurst conducts a campaign against political corruption.

John Drew makes his debut in New York.

1893 Stephen Baker is elected president of the Manhattan Company.

Thomas F. Gilroy is elected mayor of New York.

1894 The Lexow Investigation takes place in the state legislature, sifting police corruption.

Chronology

The General Removal Act, resulting from the Lexow In- *1895*
vestigation, clears out the corrupt police judges of New
York City.

The eastern part of the present Bronx Borough is annexed
to New York City.

The Harlem Ship Canal is opened.

The vogue of the drawings of Charles Dana Gibson, a
New York artist, begins, creating the "Gibson Girl," a
type of American beauty.

William R. Hearst buys the "New York Morning Journal"
and transforms it later into the "New York American."

William L. Strong is elected mayor.

Theodore Roosevelt is made police commissioner.

The Washington Arch in Washington Square is dedicated.
Colonel G. S. Waring is appointed head of the Street
Cleaning Department and revolutionizes it with the in-
auguration of his "white wings."

Columbia College becomes a university and in the follow- *1896*
ing year moves to its present location.

The Greater New York Bill is passed by the state legislature, annexing to Manhattan and the Bronx the territory now comprising the boroughs of Richmond, Brooklyn and Queens. A commission is appointed to draw up a
charter for the new city.

William R. Hearst begins the "New York Evening Journal."

The Aquarium is opened.

Grant's Tomb on Riverside Drive is dedicated. *1897*
The Merchants' Association is formed.

The first trolley car crosses Brooklyn Bridge.

The Waldorf-Astoria Hotel at Fifth Avenue and Thirty-
fourth Street is completed. (Demolished in 1929.)

Maude Adams makes her debut in New York.

The new Delmonico's restaurant is opened at Forty-
fourth Street and Fifth Avenue.

1898   Greater New York is established, an Art Commission is created and Robert Van Wyck is elected the first mayor of the greater city.

The Harlem Speedway is opened.

Theodore Roosevelt and Leonard Wood organize the "Rough Riders," a troop of volunteer cavalry, upon the United States' declaration of war with Spain.

Theodore Roosevelt is elected governor of the state of New York.

1899   The Bronx Zoological Gardens open.

A mammoth reception is held for Admiral Dewey upon his return from the Spanish-American War.

The first annual automobile parade is held in New York on Fifth Avenue.

1900   Subway construction begins in New York, the first spadeful of earth being turned by the mayor in front of the City Hall.

The first automobile road race is held on Long Island.

The first automobile show is held in Madison Square Garden.

The cornerstone of the Soldiers' and Sailors' Monument on Riverside Drive is laid by Theodore Roosevelt.

The Floradora Sextette appears in New York.

The twenty-six story Park Row Building is erected, the tallest in the world.

Schumann-Heink makes her debut in New York.

1901   John D. Rockefeller establishes the Institute for Medical Research.

Upon the death of President McKinley, Theodore Roosevelt becomes President of the United States.

Elevated railway tracks are installed on Brooklyn Bridge.

J. Pierpont Morgan establishes the billion dollar United States Steel Corporation.

Chronology

The Flatiron Building is completed.   *1902*
Prince Henry of Prussia visits New York.
The Williamsburg Bridge over the East River is opened.
Seth Low is elected mayor of New York.
Nicholas Murray Butler is elected president of Columbia
University.

The Saint Gaudens' statue of General Tecumseh Sherman *1903*
in Plaza Square is unveiled.
Enrico Caruso makes his debut at the Metropolitan Opera
House in "Rigoletto."
Andrew H. Green, "The Father of Greater New York,"
is assassinated by a crazed negro boy.
All immigration records are broken by the influx of 857,-
046 foreigners into New York.
The Stock Exchange Building, at Broad and Wall Streets,
is completed.
The city purchases the Jumel Mansion for a Museum.

George B. McClellan is elected mayor.   *1904*
The New York subway system opens from City Hall to
West 145th Street.
The first tube of the McAdoo Tunnels opens to Jersey
City (completed in 1909).
The "General Slocum" disaster occurs in the East River,
the burning of an excursion schooner, chartered by a
Sunday school organization, causing the loss of a thousand
lives.
The Lenox Avenue subway opens.

The city charter is amended to provide for a four-year *1905*
term for mayor, comptroller and borough heads.
The British Squadron under Prince Louis of Battenberg
visits New York.
Mark Twain celebrates his seventieth birthday at a dinner
at Delmonico's restaurant.

1906 Fraunces' Tavern is reconstructed according to its appearance at the time of Washington.

1907 The Custom House in Bowling Green is completed.
Mary Garden makes her New York debut in "Thais."

1908 The Pennsylvania Railroad Tunnel is opened.
The East River Tunnel connecting lower Manhattan with Brooklyn is completed.
The Fifth Avenue Association is formed.
The present Academy of Music in Brooklyn opens.
The Martyrs' Monument in Fort Greene, Washington Park, Brooklyn, is dedicated, commemorating the victims of the Wallabout prison ships of the Revolution.

1909 The Queensborough and Manhattan Bridges are completed over the East River.
The Hudson-Fulton Celebration is held in New York with a great international naval pageant on the Hudson River. Wilbur Wright makes a thrilling airship flight up the Hudson River from Governor's Island to Grant's Tomb.
The Metropolitan Life Insurance Building on Madison Square is completed.
The Grand Concourse is opened in the Bronx.
James G. Bennett II presents the Fort Washington Monument at West 183rd Street, to the city.

1910 William J. Gaynor is elected mayor.
The Pennsylvania Terminal Station is completed.
Glenn Curtiss lands at Governor's Island, after an Albany-to-New York flight by airplane.

1911 The Hall of Records, in City Hall Park, is completed.
The New York Public Library, established by joining the Astor, Lenox and Tilden bequests, is opened on Fifth Avenue and Forty-second Street.

The battleship, "New York," the largest in the world, is *1912*
launched at the Brooklyn Navy Yard.

The Altman bequest, the largest single art collection
donated, is given to the Metropolitan Museum of Art.

Mayor Gaynor dies as the result of an assassin's bullet, *1913*
and Adolph L. Kline completes his term.

The Municipal Building on Park Row is completed.

The Grand Central Terminal is completed at Forty-
second Street.

John Purroy Mitchel is elected mayor.   *1914*

The Federal Reserve Bank is established in New York.

The Panama Canal is opened, providing a new waterway
from New York to the Pacific Coast.

Ambrose Channel is completed.

The blue, white and orange city flag is adopted, the colors *1915*
of Maurice, Prince of Orange in the time of Hudson.

The German submarine, "Deutschland," makes a first
visit to New York. It is seized on a second visit in 1916
and interned during the war.

New York entertains a delegation of twenty merchants
from China.

The Sheepshead Bay Speedway on Long Island is opened.

Alexander Graham Bell talks from New York over the
telephone to San Francisco.

Permanent lighting is installed in the Statue of Liberty. *1916*

President Woodrow Wilson is re-elected, defeating Charles
Evans Hughes of New York by a few votes.

The Catskill water system, an engineering feat rivalling *1917*
the Panama Canal and calculated to supply New York
with an adequate water supply, is completed and opened
with ceremonies.

The United States declares war on Germany and New

York becomes the chief port of embarkation for the American Expeditionary Forces.

The subway from Manhattan Bridge through Canal Street as far as Union Square, is completed.

1918 John F. Hylan is elected mayor.

Regular air service is instituted between New York and Washington.

Charles M. Schwab of New York is made head of the Emergency Fleet Corporation.

President Wilson leads the Fourth Liberty Loan Parade down Fifth Avenue.

An epidemic of Spanish influenza spreads through the city.

Former Mayor John Purroy Mitchel enlists in the Army Aviation Service and is killed in an accident at the Lake Charles Aviation Field, Louisiana.

The Manhattan Company effects a merger with the Bank of the Metropolis in Union Square, acquiring its first branch office in New York City.

New York celebrates the return of peace, on November 7, in a false "Armistice Day," as the result of an erroneous press message, and on November 11 when the verified news is received.

1919 Daily air mail to Chicago is established.

New York welcomes each returning division of the A. E. F., the most notable parades being held in honor of the 369th Infantry (colored) the 27th Division, the 77th Division, and General Pershing at the head of the First Division.

The Navy plane, NC-4 flies from New York to Plymouth, England, in the first trans-Atlantic flight.

Captain Alcock, making the first non-stop trans-Atlantic flight, arrives in New York.

Theodore Roosevelt dies at his home in Oyster Bay. His birthplace, 28 East 20th Street, has since been made a national museum.

The Aviation Squad of the New York Police Department is established.

The Clark Street Tunnel is completed to Brooklyn.

New York is host to a succession of notable personages, among them the Prince of Wales, the royal family of Belgium, Prince Aage of Denmark, Cardinal Mercier of Belgium, Herbert Hoover and Premier Briand of France.

The Manhattan Company completes a merger with the *1920* Bank of Long Island, by which it acquires thirteen local offices on Long Island.

The Manhattan Company completes a merger with the Merchants' Bank at 42 Wall Street, thus making one institution of two banks that were rivals in the time of Aaron Burr and Alexander Hamilton.

$850,000 is appropriated by the government for the improvement of Jamaica Bay Channel.

A bomb explosion in which thirty-three persons are killed and over three hundred wounded occurs near the corner of Wall and Broad Streets.

Port Authority is established, giving uniformity to the *1921* solution of harbor problems over the entire area surrounding New York Bay.

A "liberty pole" is erected in City Hall Park on the site of the original one of the Revolutionary period.

Brooklyn's memorial dedicated to the city's soldier dead in the Great War is unveiled in Prospect Park.

Marshal Foch visits New York.

The first wireless communication is set up between New *1922* York and Paris.

General Joffre and Premier Clemenceau visit New York.

The first aircraft exhibition is held on Staten Island.

The Building Code, making new specifications in regard *1923* to "set back" architecture, is adopted in New York.

Lloyd George visits New York.

The Greater City holds a silver jubilee at the Grand Central Palace.

New York receives its first radio broadcast from England.

Delmonico's famous restaurant closes.

Eleanora Duse makes her New York debut at the Metropolitan Opera House.

1924 A bronze tablet presented by New York to the City of York in England is unveiled in the Guild Hall in the latter city.

Rodman Wanamaker presents to the city the Perpetual Light Memorial in Madison Square Park in commemoration of the city's soldier dead in the Great War.

The Museum of the City of New York is installed in the Gracie Mansion on the East River.

Archbishop Hayes of New York is elevated to the rank of Cardinal.

New York City opens its municipal broadcasting station.

The Manhattan Company effects a merger with the First Federal Foreign Banking Association.

1925 The Bronx River Parkway is opened.

A total eclipse of the sun is witnessed in New York.

The Fifth Royal Highlanders (the Black Watch) parade in New York on Memorial Day.

Night airmail is established between New York and Chicago.

Madison Square Garden is closed, and demolished.

1926 The first telephone conversation is held between New York and London.

New York welcomes Lieutenant-Commander R. E. Byrd and Floyd Bennett after their successful airplane flight to the North Pole.

The Queensborough Subway opens.

Chronology

Gertrude Ederle of New York, the first woman to swim the English Channel, is given a welcome in New York.

The Crown Prince and Princess of Sweden visit New York.

The Honorable James J. Walker, former member of the State Assembly from New York, is elected mayor.

Staten Island celebrates a sesqui-centennial dedication of the Billop House at Tottenville with a pageant and fireworks, commemorating the first peace negotiations held there during the Revolution.

Radio telephone service to England is established. *1927*

The Holland Vehicular Tunnel under the Hudson River is opened.

New York welcomes Captain Charles A. Lindbergh after his epochal solo flight from New York to Paris.

The dirigible "Los Angeles" flies over the city, ending the first trip of a dirigible across the Atlantic.

The Manhattan Company effects mergers with the Greenpoint National Bank and the Bank of Washington Heights.

Stephen Baker resigns from the presidency of the Manhattan Company and is elected chairman of the board of directors. Park A. Rowley is made vice-chairman of the board. J. Stewart Baker is elected president of the company.

The Arthur Kill bridges connecting Staten Island to New *1928* Jersey are completed.

The Graf Zeppelin arrives in New York, completing the first commercial trans-Atlantic flight.

Field-Marshal Allenby, who captured Jerusalem for the British during the Great War, visits New York.

The New York Medical Center is dedicated.

Mergers are effected between the Manhattan Company and the following institutions: the Bayside National Bank, the Flushing National Bank, the Queens-Bellaire Bank, the First National Bank of Whitestone, Long Island, the Bronx Borough Bank and the First National Bank of Brooklyn.

A consolidation of interests, which preserves the separate identity of both banks, is also effected with the International Acceptance Bank, Inc., of which Paul M. Warburg is chairman of the board, and F. Abbot Goodhue is president.

Construction is begun on the Fort Lee Bridge over the Hudson River, the longest single span bridge in the world.

1929 Ground is broken on Fifth Avenue and 103rd Street for the new building of the Museum of the City of New York.

The International Manhattan Company, Incorporated, with James P. Warburg as president, is organized jointly by the Manhattan Company and the International Acceptance Bank, Inc.

The Graf Zeppelin pays a second visit to New York in its record-making round-the-world flight.

Prime Minister J. Ramsay MacDonald of England pays a visit to New York.

Construction is begun at 40 Wall Street on "the tallest office building in the world," to occupy most of the block bounded by Wall, William, Nassau and Pine Streets. This edifice, known as The Manhattan Company Building, is to be the new home of The Manhattan Company, including the main offices of the Bank of Manhattan Trust Company, International Acceptance Bank, Inc. and International Manhattan Company, Incorporated.

Ceremonies are held inaugurating the construction of the Tri-Borough Bridge, connecting Manhattan Island with the Bronx and Long Island.

New York joins in a nation-wide "Golden Jubilee" celebration of Thomas A. Edison's practical application of the incandescent light to commercial purposes.

After several years of mounting prices and a country-wide fever of speculation, the New York Stock Exchange and other markets are swept by what is characterized as a "psychological panic." Billions of dollars in market values disappear within a few days.

Chronology

On November 6, stockholders of The Manhattan Company approve plans for the reorganization of its capital structure in order that it may operate more freely under its original charter of 1799 and participate more actively in the growing movement toward group banking throughout the country. Under this plan the historic Manhattan Company becomes a holding company and the owner of all the stocks of its constituent companies. Its chief officers are Paul M. Warburg, Chairman of the Board of Directors, J. Stewart Baker, Chairman of the Executive Committee and Park A. Rowley, President. Its authorized capital is increased from $22,250,000 to $40,000,000. Another feature of the plan is that the name of the Bank of the Manhattan Company is changed to Bank of Manhattan Trust Company, the officers of which are Stephen Baker, Chairman of the Board of Directors, Park A. Rowley, Vice Chairman, and J. Stewart Baker, President. Other constituent units of The Manhattan Company at this time are International Acceptance Bank, Inc. and International Manhattan Company, Incorporated.

The Honorable James J. Walker is elected for a second term as Mayor of New York City.

PRINTED IN U. S. A.

TAVERN TOPICS PRESS, INC.
LONG ISLAND CITY - NEW YORK